AF579180

STARS IN A DARK NIGHT

Ivor Gurney (1890 – 1937)

STARS IN A DARK NIGHT

The letters of Ivor Gurney to the Chapman Family

For Ken and Norma,
With Very Best Wishes
Tony Boden

Anthony Boden

with a Foreword by
Michael Hurd

ALAN SUTTON
1986

Alan Sutton Publishing Limited
30 Brunswick Road
Gloucester GL1 1JJ

First published 1986

British Library Cataloguing in Publication Data

Gurney, Ivor
Stars in a dark night: the letters of Ivor Gurney
to the Chapman Family 1914–1919.
1. Gurney, Ivor–Biography 2. Poets, English—
20th century—Biography 3. Composers—
England—Biography.
I. Title II. Boden, Anthony
780′.92′4 PR6013.U693Z/

ISBN 0-86299-225-7

Typesetting and origination by
Alan Sutton Publishing Limited
Printed in Great Britain

For Anne

Kitty, Micky, Arthur and Winnie.
Drawing by Clara Simmons, 1912

FOREWORD

In one of his shortest but most moving poems, Ivor Gurney wrote prophetically: 'There are bright tracks / Where I have been.' Yet even he, I think, would have been astonished at how bright and glowing those tracks were to become. When he died, on 26 December 1937, the prospects seemed dim indeed. But friends who knew him and believed in him as a composer and poet, kept faith and in their turn inspired those who could only know him through his work – though to know an artist through his work is to know him as he would wish to be known. Now, with nearly one hundred magnificent songs (many of them recorded), a splendidly authoritative collection of over three hundred poems, a volume of his War Letters, and a full-scale biography to hand, he suddenly appears in his true light as one of the most important figures of his generation – a creative genius of rare quality, and a singularly attractive human being.

Although the facts of Gurney's life are undeniably tragic, it should be remembered that he had a genius for friendship and a great capacity to enjoy his friends. That aspect of his life has remained somewhat in the shadows for lack of any great weight of documentary evidence. But Anthony Boden's newly discovered collection of his letters to the Chapman family restores the balance. They are not letters of worldly consequence, but, more importantly, the record of warmth and human kindness, quiet courage and dignity of spirit – written, for our delight, with a musician's ear and a poet's sensibility.

MICHAEL HURD

West Liss, Hampshire

ACKNOWLEDGEMENTS

I would like to thank: Michael Hurd, P.J. Kavanagh, David Johnston, Mrs Joy Finzi and Christian Wilson for their encouragement, help and advice; The Trustees of the Imperial War Museum, London, for the right to publish the six photographs taken in France during the First World War; Mrs Gwynneth Hargreaves for the photograph of Chosen Hill; Mr and Mrs I.M. Fraser for permission to photograph their home (St Michael's, High Wycombe); Ivan Sparkes, the Librarian at High Wycombe for the photograph of Christ Church; Chatto and Windus Ltd for permission to quote from the late Leonard Clark's Bibliographical Note to *The Poems of Ivor Gurney 1890–1937*; The Oxford University Press for permission to quote six poems from P.J. Kavanagh's *Collected Poems of Ivor Gurney*; and J.R. Haines, the Trustee of the Estate of Ivor Gurney, for consent to have access to the Gurney material in the Archives of the Gloucester City Library and for permission to publish.

CONTENTS

The Immortal Hour

(To Winnie)

I HAVE forgotten where the pleasure lay
In resting idle in the summer weather,
Waiting on Beauty's power my spirit to sway,
Since Life has taken me and flung me hither;

Here where gray day to day goes dully on,
So evenly, so grayly that the heart
Not notices nor cares that Time is gone
That might be jewelled bright and set apart.

And yet, for all this weight, there stirs in me
Such music of Joy when some perceivèd flower
Breaks irresistible this crust, this lethargy,
I burn and hunger for that immortal hour

When Peace shall bring me first to my own home,
To my own hills; I'll climb and vision afar
Great cloud-fleets line on line up Severn come,
Where winds of Joy shall cleanse the stain of war.

INTRODUCTION

'Lend me your back, Winnie!'

Such was the request made by Ivor Gurney of his young companion as they walked through Burnham Beeches one day in 1919. Winnie stopped and offered her back as a writing-surface, just as she had done many times before on those long country walks with Ivor which she enjoyed so much. Taking a small music manuscript book from his pocket he began silently to write down what he had been composing in his head. Winnie felt the gentle pressure on her back; and felt too a pride in the companionship of this man. She was nineteen years old and he twenty-eight. As he finished he whispered quietly, 'One day I shall be famous, Winnie.'

This small incident was never forgotten by Winifred Miles (nee Chapman) whose affection for Ivor Gurney remained unfaded to the end of her life in 1982.

Gurney was not to enjoy fame in his lifetime. His biographer, Michael Hurd[1] has described the upbringing and life of the man who was blessed with rare gifts as both poet and composer, especially of songs; whose joyous spirit, for the last fifteen years of his life, was abandoned to the torment of an asylum.

Ivor Gurney was born in Gloucester in 1890. The old cathedral city and the beautiful Severn valley around it inspired his natural creative genius. He was the second child of four. His father was a tailor and his mother helped in the family business. Neither of

1. *The Ordeal of Ivor Gurney* by Michael Hurd (OUP) 1978, paperback 1984.

Mr Edward Chapman – 'Le Comte'

them understood their young son, and Ivor sought friendship outside the home circle from an early age.

A stroke of good fortune occurred when Canon Alfred Cheeseman of All Saints Church, Gloucester, agreed to become Ivor's God-father – because, apart from Ivor's parents, he was the only person at the child's christening. Fortunately Canon Cheeseman took his responsibilities seriously and made it his business to introduce the young Gurney to fine poetry and prose. Ivor joined the choir of All Saints Church, where it soon became obvious that he had musical ability. Then, in 1902, he secured a place in the Cathedral Choir and began full-time education at the King's School, Gloucester.

The interest kindled by Cheeseman in music and literature was now fuelled with lessons in piano, theory and harmony, all eagerly absorbed by Gurney. He loved cricket, football and hockey and enjoyed the musical life of the school and the cathedral. However, his fellow pupils noticed a certain eccentricity in him and he was made to endure their taunts of 'batty' Gurney. In 1906 Gurney became articled to Dr Brewer, the organist at the Cathedral and remained there until 1911. In these years he met his life-long friends, Herbert Howells and the poet F.W. Harvey.

In 1911 Gurney was awarded a scholarship in Composition at the Royal College of Music, where he studied with Sir Charles Villiers Stanford. In May of that year he met Miss Marion Scott, editor of the R.C.M. magazine, who was to become a tireless advocate on his behalf for the rest of his life.

It may well have been Marion Scott who helped Gurney to obtain the organ post at Christ Church, High Wycombe, which he held both before and after the Great War. It was this appointment which gave him an escape every weekend from his dingy lodging in Fulham and through which he met the Chapman family, to whom all the letters in this book are addressed.

Edward Chapman had worked his way up in the rank ladder of the Great Western Railway until, in 1913, he was appointed Chief Clerk to the Goods Manager at Paddington Station. He moved his family from Ealing to High Wycombe where they took up residence in a solid Victorian semi-detached house called 'St.

Mrs Matilda Chapman – 'La Comtesse'

Michael's' in Castle Hill (now re-named 'The Greenway'). He was a sensitive and highly intelligent man with a determination to do his very best for his family, and he worked hard to that end. He was Churchwarden of Christ Church and, on meeting the shy new organist, was quick to offer Gurney the hospitality of his home each weekend; he even tried to secure a position on the G.W.R. for him.

Mrs Matilda Chapman seems to have been the epitome of an Edwardian lady. She was respected by her neighbours and deeply loved by her family. She set great store by her position in society and went to some expense to maintain it. When she quarrelled with Mr Chapman it was usually about money. She held Christian virtue highly and was an excellent cook. Her weakness appears to have been a tendency to hypochondria, and she also worried greatly about Gurney's fits of depression and mood swings. Gurney found her a stately lady and gave her the affectionate nick-name 'La Comtesse'. Consequently, Mr Chapman became 'Le Comte'.

The Chapmans had four children: Catherine (Kitty), Winifred (Winnie), Arthur and Marjorie. Because she was born in the same week that Mr and Mrs Chapman had been to see *The Mikado*, Marjorie was always called 'Micky'. When Ivor Gurney entered their lives in 1914, the ages of the Chapman children ranged from Kitty, the eldest at seventeen, to Micky, a mischievous ten year old. Although they were four very different personalities they all shared an immediate affinity with their new weekend companion.

Ivor brought to the children a wonderful mixture of fun and enlightenment which they were never to forget. There were games of cricket and ping-pong, long country walks and robust races. His talk was full of the wonder of music and literature. Winnie and Micky especially remembered him playing Bach preludes, Beethoven sonatas and reading aloud from Masefield's 'The Everlasting Mercy' to a young and enthralled audience. They also remembered the joy which Ivor shared with them whenever threads of inspiration were drawn together and, for the very first time, he played a completed composition on the little French piano in their drawing room. A favourite for them

Kitty (third from right) with cousins and friends.

Christ Church High Wycombe, now demolished.

amongst these works was his setting of W.B. Yeats' poem 'Down by the Sally Gardens'.

But not all of the talk and music at St Michael's was serious. Gurney's wonderful sense of humour brought delighted laughter from parents and children alike. The whole family, often with friends too, would gather round the piano and sing hilarious choruses to Ivor's accompaniment. A great favourite was the song 'Miss Bailey's Ghost', from the Cecil Sharp book of English Folksongs, during which Ivor would roll his eyes wildly and shiver with exaggerated fear whilst singing the 'O-ooh, Miss Bailey!' lines.

After supper Ivor would enjoy sitting by the open fire wearing an old pair of Mr Chapman's slippers, smoking a churchwarden pipe and talking. He would tell the Chapmans about his beloved Gloucestershire: of Maismore, Framilode, Minsterworth, Cranham and Chosen Hill. There would be speculation about the

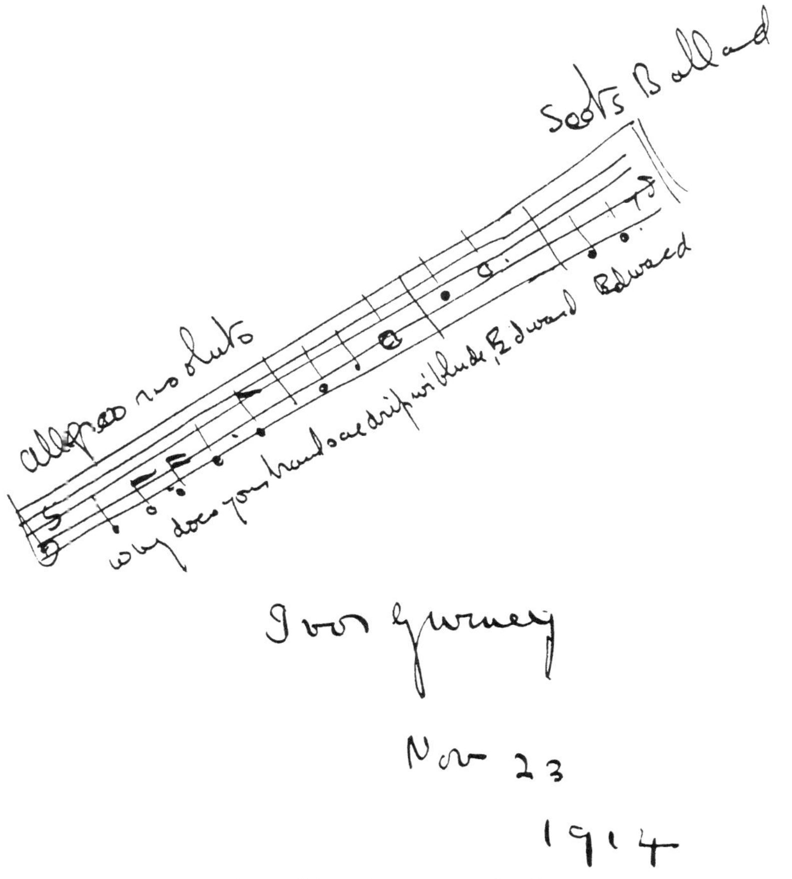

From Winnie's autograph book

outcome of the war which cast its cloud over the future of Europe and he would express his long-held belief in the United States of America as the hope for the return of stability to the world.

Determined to serve his country, in the August of 1914 Ivor volunteered for the Army but was unsuccessful. He tried again in February 1915 and this time was accepted. He returned to Gloucester and was drafted into the 2nd/5th Gloucester Regiment, 'B' Company.

There is no doubt that Ivor Gurney was a patriot; but love of

From Winnie's autograph book

country was not his only motive in wishing to serve. He knew very well the fragility of his mental health and saw in the Army his chance to gain strength to overcome the 'neurasthenia' against which he constantly struggled. In some strange way the comradeship and discipline of arms did indeed seem to provide a pause in an inevitable decline from eccentricity to insanity.

The horror and waste of war appalled Gurney and yet, experiencing the extremity of human folly, he cried out for Truth and Beauty in some of his finest verse. All the poems were sent back to Marion Scott who immediately recognised their quality and helped to arrange them into a volume which was published by Sidgwick and Jackson in 1917 under the title of 'Severn and Somme'.

In the trenches Gurney's creative energy was channelled into the writing of verse, there being very little opportunity for musical composition. Even so, several lovely songs were written, including two which perfectly expressed his yearning for the countryside of Gloucestershire and home. They are 'In Flanders', a setting of the poem by his best friend, Will Harvey, and quoted to the Chapmans in one of the letters in this collection, and 'Severn Meadows', the only poem of his own which Gurney set to music:

Only the wanderer
Knows England's graces,
Or can anew see clear
Familiar faces.

And who loves joy as he
That dwells in shadows?
Do not forget me quite,
O Severn meadows.

It is remarkable that this poignant and best known of Gurney's songs was written in the heat of war whilst he and his comrades sheltered from enemy fire in the only building left standing in the village of Caulincourt: a circular mausoleum.

Throughout the war Ivor Gurney was sustained by quiet home-thoughts and friendship in letters from the Chapmans. He revelled in all their domestic doings and had found with them, for perhaps the first time, 'the homelife which is so strong and sweet a stimulant to any sound art'.

Only Kitty was missing from Gurney's list of correspondents at St Michael's. In 1914 Ivor found his feelings for Kitty developing into an emotion much deeper than affection. He approached Mr Chapman but was told, albeit kindly, that Kitty was much too young to consider engagement. In any case, she was far from ready for love and had shared her fears with Winnie. Without rancour their relationship ended. In 1916 Kitty joined the Land Army and was sent first to Syde in Gloucestershire and then, in 1917 to The King's Farm at Windsor where she met her future husband.

Each summer the Chapmans rented a cottage in Perranporth, Cornwall. Winnie was a delicate child: as an infant she suffered from a 'weak chest', during one severe illness was placed in an oxygen tent and for a time, was not expected to survive. The sea air and exercise of the Perranporth holidays were of great benefit to her health and, ironically, she outlived her brother and both of her sisters. When the family set off for Perranporth in the Summer of 1915 Winnie had a secret. Hidden amongst her most treasured possessions was a tiny white envelope containing a single lock of Ivor Gurney's hair. Upon it she had written in pencil: 'My Dearest Ivor's Curl'.

All the letters and documents in this collection were found amongst the possessions of my late mother-in-law, Winifred Miles (Winnie) and of her sister, Marjorie Freeman (Micky). Winnie died in 1982 and Micky in 1979; their sister Kitty died in 1963 and their brother Arthur in 1954 whilst playing cricket.

Only very rarely did Gurney date his letters. I have attempted to assemble them in the correct order by reference to types of paper, the use of ink or pencil, postmarks on the few surviving envelopes and, in the main, content.

1
TRAINING FOR WAR

February 1915 – May 1916

GURNEY'S BATTALION MOVED FROM GLOUCESTER FIRST TO NORTHAMPTON AND THEN, IN APRIL 1915, TO CHELMSFORD, FROM WHERE THEY MADE SEVENTEEN-MILE ROUTE MARCHES TO EPPING TO WORK ON THE DEFENSIVE TRENCH SYSTEM FOR OUTER LONDON.

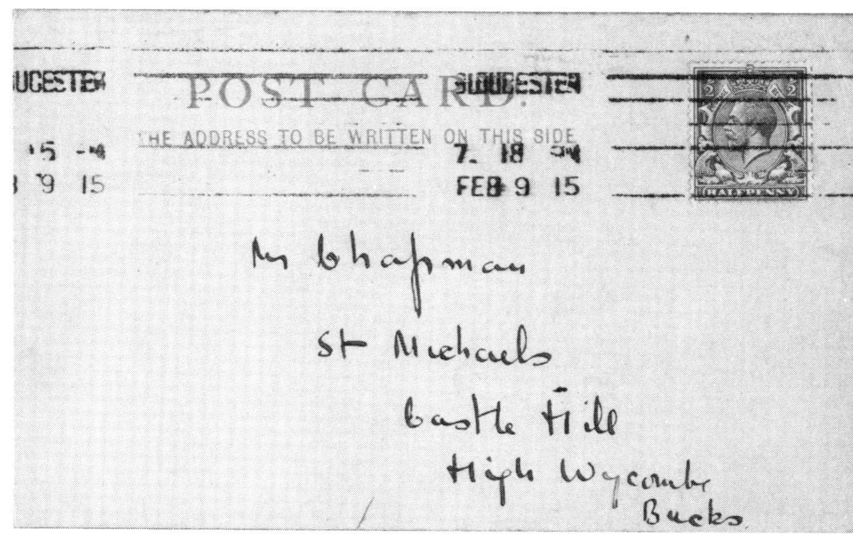
POST CARD.
THE ADDRESS TO BE WRITTEN ON THIS SIDE
GLOUCESTER
7. 18
FEB 9 15

Mr Chapman
St Michaels
Castle Hill
High Wycombe
Bucks

Private Gurney (5th Gloucester Reserve Battalion) sends you greetings.

Postcard to Mr Chapman from Gloucester dated 9th Feb, 1915.

Pte I B Gurney
B Company
2nd 5th Glosters
Northampton

My *Dear Chapman*

Well, life is distinctly harder here than at Gloucester. 1st parade 7–7.45 Physical Drill 2nd, 9–12.45 Drill 2–4.30 Drill. Hard work too, but I hang on and hope for the best. I think I shall come through. If it tires me, it tires the other recruits also and so I don't care.

I was going to send my billet address, but that is forbidden, and besides I did not like my first billet and have now changed it. You may expect an army biscuit by post soon. Personally I rather like them, and though they are terrifically hard, hot tea alters that.

I hope everbody is well and out of bed, and – oh yes! did Arthur get his Sherlock Holmes, and has he liked them? I could not find the one supposed to be left at home.

How is the ping-pong, and the hockey, and Moses and all? My thoughts go back to High Wycombe, and the ping pong tournaments 'and all' with pleasure, and the conviction that I should not be as well now if it were not for that.

I think there is no danger of my breaking down, and a large prospect of my becoming much better, thank the Lord, and paid a bob a day for it, too!

The chaps at my billet (3) are very nice and we ought to have some good evenings together. How is Mr Ketchlee? Tell him to advertise for the Lost Tribes in the Agony column of *The Times*. If the Germans answer it, then of course his theory is wrong.

Goodbye

Your affectionate friend

Ivor Gurney

Pte Ivor Gurney
6 Platoon
B Company
2nd 5th Glosters
Northampton

My *Dear Chapman*

I should have replied to that P.C. but never got it. Some of my things have gone astray to a man in this Company named J. Gurney, and he forgot to let me have it. I have not yet thanked you for the writing case – which is charming, nor the pipe lighter, which is very useful on a march; especially in a wind.

I hope the family is all right now and jolly and revelling in ping pong tournaments galore. I am afraid you will not see me this side of the war. Leave is very difficult to get, and as I was such a short time at home it must be spent there; if I get any at all. Tomorrow the foreign service men do their firing; those who pass the tests may be at the front any time soon. Our first 5th (of which we are the reserve) may go at any time, and reserves are not kept waiting long in *this* war.

Our rifles are of Japanese make, but some others are to be served out for firing – the Lee-Enfield type.

No, I am not ill. Indeed they tell me I look much better; and, indeed, I must be pretty strong for a neurastheniac. Yesterday I was on from 8.15 – 12.15, 3 – 5.30, 7.15 – 10 and then we had an alarm and turned out at 11 not to get back till 2.15.

The ordinary day is
6.45 – 7.30
8.45 – 12.30
2.00 – 4.30

This I do and am never very tired, though during last night's alarm I marched in a sort of dream, but this fatigue was healthy and not nervous exhaustion. The food has been wretched, but now is better. Half my money has gone on extra food, chiefly meat, a substance considered in the Army to be composed entirely of fat bone and gristle. I buy bully beef when it becomes too annoying. We may leave here for Chelmsford any day; and from Chelmsford perhaps – who knows? – to the Dardanelles. There are rumours . . .

Well, this is all about myself, but the details about army life are from the inside, and, chiefly, about the inside. I do not at all forget you – Pa and Ma, Kitty, Winnie and the exuberant Mickie. Not by no means. But rifles, boots, buttons, need cleaning; coats need rolling, clothes brushing; and there are night operations, street pickets, fire pickets, and guards to be done.

May you all be happy and healthy and wealthy and wise – more so every day. Good-bye to all of you. Easter is near; and after then, I am no more organist of Christ Church – my official tie to High Wycombe will be gone, and there will be left that unofficial one of being your friend.

Yours affectionately

Ivor

On back of envelope: Would you like a hay band or a straw[1] – ? I've finished with mine.

1 Simple men who were unable to distinguish right from left were given a hay band and a straw band to tie round each leg. Instead of 'right, left' the drill instructor called out: 'hay, straw!'

Pte Gurney
B Company
2nd 5th Glosters
Chelmsford, Essex

Dear Old Winnie

Thank you for your letter, and Dear Comtesse, thank you for the cake which is *good*, and dear Micky, thank you also for *your* letter.

I am sorry you poor creatures that there has been such pestilence and famine among you. And so unseasonable a thing as rheumatism; which should go with winter and plum puddings. I am writing this near Galley wood outside Chelmsford. We are on what is called anti-aircraft picket. That is – we are on the look out for Zeppelins etc. And at this time it should be exciting enough. We get out about 7 p.m. and stay till 6 a.m. In fine weather it is very good fun; both sunset and dawn are beautiful, and there is only an hour's guard each.

This will be my last till next Sunday.

Bayonet practice is over now, and we ought to have more firing soon.

How is Arthur getting on at cricket? Good scores and hat tricks I hope.

We are leaving here soon I believe, for somewhere near Epping perhaps.

Well, goodbye Winnie dear and I hope the toothache is quite well now, and Daddies rheumatics.

Love to Everybody and no rheumatism or crocking up of any kind.

Yours affectionately

Ivor

My Dear Winnie

I wonder how you too are getting on, you poor imp of misery. (This is a letter to a lady.) It is the patriotic duty of every English woman to wear a pack now, and I don't feel disposed to write politely to anyone who doesn't – and 60 lbs at least in weight. But blessings on thee. Thou art a blithesome thing, God wot. Would that it had been possible to have taught thy nimble forefinger the divine Beethoven, but the gods willed otherwise. I suppose you are looking forward to Perranporth and to see the great Atlantic rollers in a perpetual surge and attack on our England. My spirit will be with you there, chasing the bunnies or quietly watching the 'sunshot palaces high' and breathing contentment with the common air. This seems to be a frightfully high faluting letter; but you will understand it, and it is such a restful thing, to high-falute. Many of our occupations are 'so low, my dear'. But this morning I sat hidden behind a table, on my beam-ends and had a high old time learning the Morse alphabet and reading the paper. This afternoon, now at this moment, was to be given to us as a time of peace, as we are to be out all night, but They (a malison on them!) could not let us be, and ordained a hut-inspection, and of kits etc. But Private Gurney did espy the orderly corporal in the next hut, and got him outside straightway to listen at the window; whence he is now writing letters in a wood a mile away from camp – even this to his amiable correspondent, Mistress Winifred Chapman, to whom he sends his love and best wishes.
Goodbye

Yours affectionately

Ivor B.

To the Paleface Chief Arthur

Glass-eyes, the player on instruments, sends thee greeting. Prays the Great White Chief for thy welfare and desires to know the state of thy health. Announces that he has 4 or 5 loaded blanks which may arrive at Chief Arthur's wigwam at any moment, should an insurrection headed by Smith, the Rushes By[1] (the henpecked medicine man) or any such washout (keep that dark though, destroy the missive). But really old man, are you all right now? Body, soul and spirit, and between the cracks?

Here there are no more blizzards, but Spring with the sweetest smiles, and so I hope you are cricketing – on the heath or elsewhere.

But I am sure you stood what you had to pluckily as befits an Englishman. Someday we will hunt together on Keep Hill, and gather many scalps to hang round our umbrellas. Till then, Farewell and Greetings.

Yours affectionately

Ivor

POSTCARD addressed to Mr Chapman, St Michael's. etc.
dated: 8 Apr 15

I got your letter yesterday morning. It was such a pity. I should very much have liked to have seen you again – but there is a chance next week. I believe – *believe* mind, that we go to Epping Forest on Friday. I B G

1. Rev Rushby-Smith, vicar of Christ Church, High Wycombe. Mrs Rushby-Smith was the choir mistress

POSTCARD addressed to Mrs Chapman, St Michael's etc.
Dated: 21 Ap 15

Dear Comtesse

Thank you for your nice letter. As for arrangements, they must be hopelessly vague. We are reported to be leaving here either on Sat: or Monday. I heard that the Captain told our platoon so today fairly definitely. If it is true (and I think it is) we return to Chelmsford, another 17 miles! But nothing – nothing is certain, but uncertainty. I B G

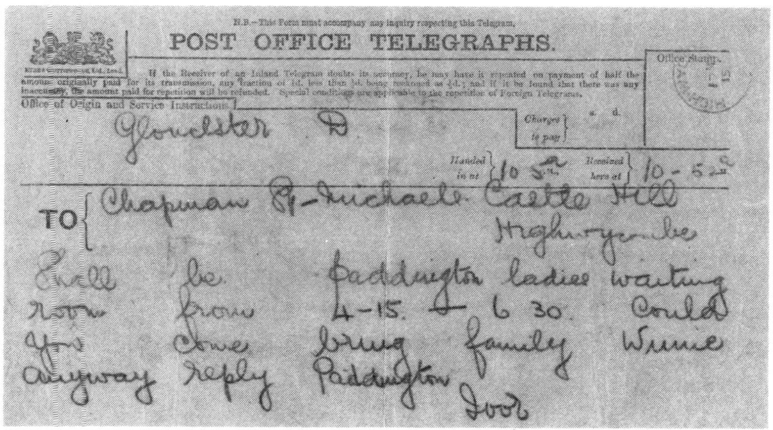
N.B.—This Form must accompany any inquiry respecting this Telegram.

POST OFFICE TELEGRAPHS.

If the Receiver of an Inland Telegram doubts its accuracy, he may have it repeated on payment of half the amount originally paid for its transmission, any fraction of 1d. less than ½d. being reckoned as ½d.; and if it be found that there was any inaccuracy, the amount paid for repetition will be refunded. Special conditions are applicable to the repetition of Foreign Telegrams.

Office of Origin and Service Instructions. Gloucester D

Charges to pay s. d.

Office Stamp.

Handed in at 10 5 Received here at 10 - 52

TO Chapman St Michaels Castle Hill Highwycombe

Shall be Paddington ladies waiting room from 4-15 6 30. Could you come bring family Winnie anyway reply Paddington Ivor

TELEGRAM

POST OFFICE TELEGRAPH

Addressed: Chapman, St Michael's, Castle Hill, High Wycombe
Dated: 17 May 15

Message: Shall be Paddington ladies waiting room from 4.15 – 6.30. Could you come bring family Winnie anyway reply Paddington Ivor

Pte Gurney
B Company
2nd 5th Glosters
Wintry Farm Camp
Epping, Essex

My Dear Chapman

We have been here in camp just over a week, and the whole time has been a rush from 5 o'clock reveille to 9.45 Lights out. The chief thing is attacks and all sorts of company and brigade actions; this is why we have come into camp. The roads are horrid, bristly with shingle and pebbles which raise blisters in record time. For breakfast we have as a rule bacon; for dinner either what they call shackles (stewed meat) or roast meat; for tea, bread, margarine, jam, and 'tea', made in the same dixie as the shackles – very different in every way to the dainty meal held about the same time at St Michael's High Wycombe. No oatcake, no scones; likewise no ping-pong. If you would like to see in camp, one is allowed to bring people in on Sundays, when the camp deletes as much of its grease as possible, ameliorates its language, and relaxes the stern visage of war.

The Bucks, the Oxford and Bucks, the Glosters, the Berks and a few Engineers and RAMC are all hereabouts, and all affable to visitors. Camp open from 3 – 9.

Has Arthur made any great scores lately? and what has Winnie done? Micky I suppose is just as naughty and nice as ever all reared on the bounteous provision prepared by the Comtesse and made possible by the arduous exertions of the Count.

Our first reinforcements have gone – three days ago; and our second are ready to go; and so the Brigade gradually dribbles out to the Front.

Well, goodbye all you dear creatures in Buckinghamshire.

Oh, does anyone want an exciting book about Scotland? *The New Road* by Neil Munro would suit.

Good bye

Your affectionate friend

Ivor Gurney

Pte Gurney
6 Platoon
2nd 5th Glosters
Epping

My *Dear Comtesse*

I am sorry that you have had so wretched a time at so unprofitable a game. It is hard lines on one who would like to live life to be cooped up in bed and see the clouds drift and do nothing and be nothing of importance.

Of course I forgive the lecture. It was deserved, though not so much as you think perhaps. The 'nice long evenings' are occasionally filled up by army duties, such as guard, street picket, night operations, fatigue. And last Monday we marched 17 miles, hunted for billets, and at 7.30, when I was about to go in, I was collared for duty and got two hours sleep, and on duty all next day. Besides, unlike yourself I hate writing. That 17 miles was with the pack – that is, about 40 lbs to carry.

We shall be here till Monday week, but whether I can get leave or no is doubtful. Of course I do not mean my 48 hours leave which would be spent in Gloucester – but leave till 12 at night. Not this Saturday anyway, but perhaps next. On Sunday I am on guard. Please thank Micky for her letter. It was just like the dear rascal, and I wish I were back to lose to Arthur and Winifred Emma the champion once again. I wish you all were not so good to me. I like my friends to be willing to give to me in proportion to what myself would give, and you are all too generous in affection and otherwise.

Hoping you are better now, with love to all

I remain

Your affectionate

Ivor Gurney

Chelmsford Essex
1915

My *Dear Comtesse*

I am very sorry, but everything has turned out a failure. On the last two Saturdays I have been inoculated and on guard, and the few hours I hoped for either yesterday or today have not been granted. I should have written before; but camp has been very hard, and when there was any spare time it was spent on the flat of my back. Reveille 5 Breakfast 6.30 Dinner 1.30 Tea 4.30 – 5.0, and on all the time between those hours!

I am sorry not to have written, but always hoped to be able to let you know I was able to get a Saturday pass. Hope you will all enjoy Perran.

Yours affectionately

Ivor

Pte Gurney
B Company 2nd 5th Glosters
Chelmsford, Essex

My Dear Winifreda

Thank you for the p.c. and your letter to which I never replied, miserable sinner that I am! Bless you my child for your friendship and thoughts of me. Now they have put me in our new brass band – on second-hand instruments – I shall have more time and in all probability become fat and lazy. ('Fat and well-liking' the Psalmist says).

I hope all you dear creatures are happy and dirty down at Perran. Why have colds? Why have minor ailments? What use are they? What cash value do they represent? What relation do they bear toward the Eternal Verities? (Carlyle, whom some day you will read).

My landlady here curiously enough stayed at Perranporth years and years ago; she loves it, and likes to speak of it. She is an individual old girl, with a mind of her own, and very kind.

I was sorry not to see you before you went, especially as it is probably the last chance. I have had no leave for about 14 weeks, and no half-day leave since I saw you all. Kitchener has now seen and passed us. We are to be ready to take our places when wanted, and so the 5 days leave preliminary to going abroad has just started, and the first batch went today. I must at least see the Comte at Paddington when my time comes, which may be in about 3 weeks time.

Don't get drowned, or sucked down by shifting sands, or get battered to bits by those huge Atlantic rollers. How are the trout?

I hope to see you all again one day, sound in body and mind, and to give you all a hundred runs and beat you, or 49 points out of 50 at ping-pong and beat you; you half-Gaelic rapscallions!

The 2nd/5th Battalion Gloucester Regiment Band in 1915.
Ivor Gurney is in the rear rank, fourth from right.

4214.

Good-bye, Winnie dear, and increase in wisdom, stature and health, and tell me all about yourself when you write. No polite inquiries!

Yours affectionately

Ivor

Pte Gurney
B Company 2nd 5th Glosters
Chelmsford, Essex

My *Dear Comtesse*

I am sorry that worries pursue you even down in Cornwall, and that the poor kids are not up to the mark. Perhaps it is all right now, and the sun is shining.

Why do you suppose that when you do not get a letter, I am 'cross'? Well, it is an old trick now, and a legitimate one; though doubtfully useful as you must realise that I don't take fits of *that* kind, anyhow.

I am glad to be able to tell you – that my mind is gradually becoming more sane and more happy. It is hard work, but now I realise to the full that it is chiefly my mind at fault, I push on that way; and feel more hopeful. But please don't praise me for my courage! It is my only chance of happiness and health.

You won't mind this bit of self-analysis I hope? It is better to do very little of it, though.

Don't overwork yourself and spoil your holiday; it is better and nobler by far to worry over other people than yourself, but why do either?

Have you got Browning at all? The second volume of Everyman is excellent; or did I give you that little red-covered volume? That is good too. You ought to get Wordsworth in that editon; it is first rate.

What must the sea look like? The sea – unbroken in force by any barriers for thousands of miles! What free grace and careless glory must show itself in such unhampered movements.

'St. Michael's'

Well, probably (by statistics and ordinary reckoning) I myself may take joy in it someday; when this tyranny is overpast.

They have made a brass band now, and for the present put me in it; on a [sic] instrument called the Baryton – a brass cornet – affair. I like it, though my lips are too thick ever to do it justice, perhaps. Still, practice may put that right.

Now go I to bathe in the Chelmer; not an imposing river; nothing of the 'rude imperious surge' about it.

Good luck!

Yours affectionately

Ivor

Pte Gurney
B Company
2nd 5th Glosters
Chelmsford, Epping

My Dear Creatures

It was good-as-gold of you to send me such a parcel of good things. Never have I felt such a sensation of overwhelming luxury and surprise of riches since (alas! many years agone; lang syne) I bought a penny lucky bag and discovered a real wooden monkey on a real wooden stick. The air cushion is not at present useful to me, but if we have to sleep out it will be a blessing unparalleled. The tin will do for baccy, stamps, stray sovereigns, maggots and beetles, small photos. What the handkerchiefs will do for is better left out. Praps some day I may find the need for soap.

I wrote a p.c. to Mr Chapman about a week ago, telling him that I should be in London at a certain time. Two days after I remembered that the address on the p.c. was Mr Chapman – Goods Manager. So that may have been the reason I did not see him. Perhaps he lost his post through the G.M.'s jealousy and so has left you down at Perranporth to live on rabbits until

Officers of the Great Western Railway Goods Department

Supplement to "GREAT WESTERN RAILWAY MAGAZINE" JANUARY 1921 PHILIP REID, FLEET ST, LONDON E.C.

he can scheme some money or other. Perhaps he's dead of grief, all through an unfortunate slip. I'm very sorry if this is so; he was a man who, though enthusiasm would be out of place, was not altogether bad: he was not as black at some points as others. His chief use was to excuse, by the display of his imperfections, any tendency to gaucherie or villany in his children. And a good excuse it was for them, on almost anything.

(Just for sentiment's sake I will light up, and accompany this letter with Winnie's etceteras pipe and baccy. Puff, puff! Thank you!).

I am very sorry to have left this letter so long. It was very wrong when there was [sic] so many nice presents to thank you for. They are all in use, save only the cushion, or rather pillow, for which, thank Goodness, no occasion for use has yet arisen.

I am afraid that your visit to Perranporth is drawing to an end. But you must draw cold comfort from the fact that High Wycombe is a very nice place to live in. Compare it with any London suburb.

My best friend[1] has just got a D.S.M. and has been recommended for a commission, but his nerves are pretty shaky. When we are to go, no one knows, but from rumours it is not likely to be just yet. But what are rumours worth?

I should like a game of ping-pong very much: it would appeal to me more than forming fours or other such manifestations of military glory.

My 5 days leave happened about a week ago, more than a week in fact; and the beauty of my own county astounded and enchanted me more than ever. As a friend of mine[2] has lately written –

1. F.W. Harvey
2. 'In Flanders' by F.W. Harvey

I'm homesick for my hills again,
My hills again!
To see above the Severn plain
Unscabbarded against the sky
The blue high blade of Cotswold lie;
And giant clouds go royally
By jagged Malvern with a train of shadows'.

Isn't it exquisite?

Good bye all you unfortunate people who weren't born there!

Yours affectionately

Ivor

Pte Gurney
Band *D* Company
etc.

P.S. Have you the Everyman Century of Essays? If so did I give it to you? If not, *please* let me have it.

My Dear Comtesse

I wonder how you like High Wycombe now? The change from Perranporth must be great, but let it not blind you to the merits of High Wycombe, which are many.

Today is bright and bracing, and after flat and featureless Essex Bucks would be Beauty personified. Walk you straight round Castle Hill and be glad of it. I hope you are pretty well and cheery after your long holiday – it was a long one you know; and you must not have wasted money by not feeling a jolly sight better.

You are quite wrong about my not wanting letters. I like

them better than for years I have (a sure sign of improving health), and am glad of them. But I *don't* like wee bits from R.M. or A.E. Benson, and sentimental 'Weltmüthings' to give you a Teutonism. They insult God and Man either by refusing to see truth, or insisting on unimportant platitudes. I like letters to be about the people who write them. 'A healthy egotism' as our German friends would say. There is a distinct possibility that we shall not go abroad till March, which will make the chances of getting through all right quite large.

My mind gradually tranquillises itself, and more and more I see what a splendid teacher Wordsworth is for all sorts of men. When I can lie quite still in joy by the side of some stream or in a meadow for an hour or more, then music will come easily and well. Not till then. Happiness is in ourselves, and until this is a platitude to be smiled at for its obviousness, it is not possible for sensitive people to be happy. Come and let's be – together. At present, it is probable that I am in front.

I find I have been preaching. Sorry! But it is as much for myself as you.

But . . . does that make it any more excusable? I wonder . . .

Yours affectionately

Ivor

Oh, Mr Smith has not replied to my letter. The one before was curt. Is this due to my attitude on Prophesy?

My Dear Kids

How's hockey? How's cats? How's dogs? How's Football? How's Keep Hill?

I would very much like to share all these with you, but Lord Kitchener won't let me. Herbert Horatio Has the Hump. But really: Essex is a flat and unsatisfactory place, and now Autumn is in the air I remember High Wycombe, and how I went down there just about this time last year, and discovered a family

Postcard to 'Messrs. Chapman' from Epping dated 9th July, 1915
Message reads:
'Why did they take Them
or
The Drunken Recruiting Officer'
(Ivor Gurney standing at far left).

which liked Bach and whose presents I am now loaded with. I take baccy from a magnificent sterling silver pouch-thing, light up a splendid Spring Model pipe, and recline on a lovely Latest style air-cushion, carefully dusting my trousers with an exquisite handkerchief embroidered (as is the cushion) with my name, and am ready to sneeze in the most gentlemanly fashion into the most lady-like handkerchiefs. Is Winnie going back to School? What will Kitty do? Is Arthur going to take a commission? Is Micky allowed to associate with other more respectable children?

How's Dad? With whom I used to settle the fate of Europe

and the Universe with my feet pointing upwards to the skies, as the hymn says.

Mr Jack White is in the Naval Air service now, and has made trips into the empyrean (Gotcher!)

Oh, dear! but how sick we are of the army; and how we watch the placards for any indication of a near end to the war. Things are rosy just at present, rosier than they were, anyhow. It's Sunday, today, and were things different from what they are, I might be looking forward to clutching hold of about 6 pairs of hands and trying not to break my neck, *and* look affable! Do you remember how the Gadarene swine used to run down the quarry at Keep Hill? Well, one day again perhaps . . .

Good bye everybody

Your affectionate friend

Ivor

My *Dear Micky*

I hope you have been doing no *very* naughty things lately, you imp of iniquity, you! How many times have you fallen in, and upset the whole household for clean clothes? How many dogs have you worried, you extreme example of wilful perversity? How many cats? Children? Mothers? Sisters? Brothers? Aunts? But indeed, I may be quite sure that it will take more than a European war, and a wetting to damp *your* spirits and stop *you* dancing. Go on then, be naughty and get muddy. It is not I that have to set things straight. They may scold, but I am far enough away not to mind so much, and all I want is a letter about it, and kisses at the end.

Draw me a picture, lady-artist. Make me a song. Play tricks – and – naughtiness all the day long.

Yours affectionately

Ivor B:

Pte Gurney etc

My Dear Old People

You'll not have me with you, I fear, just yet. Never mind, I don't care whether it's Xmas day or not, you shall have me with you before very long, as we are getting leave in bits. My bit will probably not be very long delayed. I only hope you rackety kids won't be at school when the auspicious occasion ausps.

Remember me in thy down-sitting and thy uprising. At the pinging of the pong, and the rendering on the tinkles. Sing you loud and lustily, and use your windbags bustily; prostrate yourselves every five minutes, reverently murmuring 'I.B.G.', and no doubt something will reward you; though the time be long-distant, and its connection with the act doubtful and hard to trace.

Bless you, my children
(From 60 downwards)

Your affectionate

I.B.G.

Pte Gurney
2/5 Glosters
Chelmsford

My Dear Comtesse

I thoroughly expected to be with you today, but we are on Brigade duties, and have had so many extra things to do that I did not think it worth while to apply – rightly, as it turned out. But either next Saturday or Sunday will do I think. Probably Saturday – as I could stay till 10, if there is a train then. You say it is a pleasure to see me. I suppose it is difficult for a person outside the army to know what a delight the mere being absent from quarters is. And when the return is to delicate food, white tablecloths, large, or largish rooms, and such company as I can get at High Wycombe, then the feeling lasts as much as a week, and one is able to stand a whole 7 days without too much remembering the feeling of utter futility and waste of time that is the average thought of any educated man in Army life. I am not at all sure that we shall not be glad to get abroad – glad for a time anyhow; and that seems to be coming not long after Xmas.

Thank you, Madam; the food is better now. Indeed, I have left quite a lot lately. It is to be hoped your progeny (there's an expression to be applied to such children!) are either well or on the mend now.

As for winter trees – I believe, never are they so beautiful as now. Never are afterglows so far beyond words to describe as in Winter. And never is teatime so lovely a thing to be looked forward to – or regretted most in the Army.

But I don't grumble. My health improves all the time. I am fit for double as much as when I joined 9 months ago. My mind can escape from itself a little. I think of music with some pleasure, and in another 6 months I ought to (be) able clearly to see my way to such health of mind and body as never before. Why not you, too? It is a question of thought and not overworking and Joy consciously created till the creation becomes habitual and spontaneous. And as for worrying – If the maker of Stars and Waters and Trees does not know his business, I am afraid that there is no one who can teach him.

Goodbye, and best of luck. O, I forgot to mention the Railway job. I am afraid it will be very difficult as there are only 612 of us. That is to say only 12 more can leave. But I never worry about possibilities, or hardly ever.

Yours affectionately

Ivor

On reverse of envelope Gurney has written 'Letter and Mittens just received thank you!'

Pte Gurney
2/5 Glosters
Chelmsford

Banc. D. Co:

My Decr Comte (de Tilda) = title of female successor

The Comtesse your gracious consort has written me a charming letter all about herself (and myself), but happens to mention that you would like a letter from me; and as it is rather important to me to keep in with you, I take the hint, though there is not much to say.

There was no train from London that night, and so after sleeping for an hour or two at a Soldiers and Sailors home – a most comfy 3*d* doss – I went down to prison on the paper train at 5 a.m.

When we (for there were other daredevils besides myself) handed our passes in, the following dramatic scene occurred – from the Play 'An Escape from Gehenna'.

Act I Hurried evasion
Act II High Wycombe
Act III Doss house in London slums
Act IV Handing the Pass In
Scene Quarter Guard Room
(Enter two men of doubtful mien and hangdog air)
1st Guard: Hullo!
1st Criminal: Ah do! Where's the Sergeant?
1st Guard: There
1st Criminal: Thanks . . . Sorry, Sergeant, to wake you up. Here they are.
Sergeant: (Grunt . . . Grunt . . . Grunt . . .) Ere, wot's this?'
1st and 2nd Criminal: Wot's Wot?
Sergeant: 'Ere, wot's this?'
1 & 2 Criminal: Wot's Wot? Sergeant?
Sergeant: This! Wot's this? These are midnight passes
1st Criminal: Ah, yes . . . most unfortunate. Most

unfortunate. Somehow or other there didn't happen to be a train after 8.30. They must have taken 'em off. Bit rotten, wasn't it . . . We didn't mean to disturb you. Very sorry. Won't do it again. Quite a mistake.

Sergeant: Ah . . . Well you just get off into your billets at once. There 'ud be a blushing row if anybody seen you.

1 & 2 Criminal: Oh yes . . . thanks, Sergeant. Good morning.

Exeunt

Act V *has not yet come, and doesn't look like it.*

It was good to get back to St Mike's again, bless it, and feel free and golopshus once again.

We went out on a brigade stunt, and got a dinner of bone splinters and hot water at 4 o'clock next day; so the impression of cloistral peace was heightened by contrast. Curious that a rotten liver should be able to spoil everything save only memories . . .

The Comtesse says you are in Wales, and have not yet seen the miracle-working gent who may be able to recall me, like Orpheus, from Hell. That doesn't affect me much . . I do not dare to hope much for fear . . .

But if it is real, and not phantasmal and only a rosy dream, let the proof be forthcoming not too late. I may be snatched away of a sudden into some remote outlandish place outside England, but that is not immediately likely, though there are rumours.

I might also say that if there is another place, Cridlan that analyst etc. from Stevens (*sic*) Jammery[1] would be delighted to get it, and would if necessary get references from his uncles. He would certainly be very useful. Well, that's all about that – FOR THE PRESENT I hope.

Oh, but this is a grey unuseful unbeautiful waste, this Essex. No suns, etc, no colours. No beechy hills, no downs, no

1. Stephens Jam factory in Gloucester

nothing, no kids to play with, no free cigarettes, no ping-pong. No something that gives romance and mystery to ordinary trees and hedges and houses in more fortunate parts. If ever I come to write music some of it will be around Totteridge, Keep Hill, and that Macbeth-like wood that lies beyond it to the south. Some of it also around the homelife which is so strong and sweet a stimulant to any sound art.

But this is rather gassy. Get me out of this. Let me know that I shall still be doing war-duty with a practical certainty of being some day able to do all that lies in me, some day, for the honour of England; which is very dear to me. Indeed, if I could feel certain that there never would be anything in me really worth the showing in music, the first thing I'd do would be to volunteer where they wanted me most. Though on that point even, I believe that the Railway Transport, if there is a chance to rise, will give me a fair run.

Please excuse this egoistical letter, but I can write no others that are not washy platitudes.

Yours affectionately

Ivor Gurney

POSTCARD

To Mrs Chapman, St Michael's, High Wycombe, Bucks.
Dated by postmark 22 Oct 15

Sorry not to have answered your letters, but ever since Monday we have been out on manoeuvres: and civilisation a thing unknown.

I have made application for Sunday leave, but shall not know till then whether I shall get it. If you knew what a time we have had this past 3 weeks you would not suspect any sane person of not wishing to get anywhere else. But I'm afraid you'll have to pay for it. I.B.G

The Chapmans' holiday cotttage at Perranporth, Cornwall.
A watercolour by G.F. Beckett

My Dear Old Winnie

I am sorry you have been sick and at such an untactful time of holidays. Perhaps it is all better now. Bless you my child, I hope so. As for the photo, it simply hasn't arrived, and my laziness has prevented me writing to know why.

I hope to see you next Sunday, and it is fairly certain that I shall – or on Saturday.

What a funny Xmas this will be! Away from everything in the way of Children and ping-pong. Anyway, I shall be feeling much better this year than last, and not such a drag on the entertainment as then; for we simply must get up some sort of entertainment in this dead-alive unfortunate hole. Either 4 or 8 of us are plotting how to make believe that army life may be made jolly about Christmas time. We'll do it, somehow. Unless they stick us on guard, or the extremely military operation of picking up paper. Anyway, I hope all you will concentrate all your phsycic [sic] faculties on having a damgood time then; and remembering me only to pledge me in the quaffing of huge tankards of beer, to the shouts of Waeshael! Let the ancestral hall of St Michael, and its stately keep and barbican echo to the sound.

Epic on *the Celebration of the Mass of Christ*

Kinkering Kongs
Do ping their pongs.
And title-takers
Get stomach achers.

Tell tales all round again. Put your hand on each others backs, and count the shivers. Judge each ghost tale, not only by the frequency of the shivers but also by their duration and wobblyness.

Goodbye dear and best wishes

Yours affectionately

Ivor

Winnie, Micky a friend and the Chapman family dog Barry on the beach at Perranporth.

POSTCARD WITH PHOTOGRAPH addressed to Messrs Chapman and Co
Dated: 17 Dec.

Merry Xmas and don't forget last year's ping pong and beeeeastly wet, Likewise especially I.B.G.

Mr Dear Old Win:

O don't be sick, seedy, out of sorts and so on, for soon it is the intention of the famous composer to visit the Hill of the Castle with St Mike's situated thereon (its outhouses and messuages pertaining) and to find you not in a condition to play Ping Pong would be sad indeed. Well, here's to a Happy New Year to you and all the rest with no crock-up and nothing but robust and even noisy health.

It's snowing hard outside. Snowing like blazes (to use an unsuitable simile) and lovely to look at the dark-sky world is. Can you send any hints on how to pack shirts, music, socks, books, coats, shoes, of enormous bulk into a box half the size of the combined mass? If so please do, for that is the problem that confronts me. Or hints how to write joyous masterpieces when in the dumps? Ah, but you poor dear, having to lie still, and take things what they call 'easy' have none too good a time. May it pass, soon, soon! Dear Kid, I am so glad you like that book. It is an honour to get in with such a select crowd, ain't it? Book 2 of me is at the publishers but no reply has been received as yet. Well, here's hopes to see the whole Joyful Crowd of you soon.

With love from your humble obedt servant

I.B.G.

My Dear Comtesse

This kindness comes from all of you, but it bears the special mark of Tildaness upon it. Kindness follows me through life, and I can say at least this for myself, that it bewilders me, and makes me shy. But you must be doing these things, I suppose. Thank you very much indeed.

As my letter says, the Family letter, I hope to see you soon and to get an oasis of green in this dreary-same life. But I keep pretty cheery, and have no doubt you are practising the noble art of keeping your pecker up. Anyway, let's all hope you will all keep well and happy in this coming New Year. What would not the end of the war and a week or so at Wycombe mean to me? Nevertheless, we cultivate the habit of slummocking along without worry and smiling at Life. Oatcake is no contemptible help to this, nor Wordsworth either.

Thank you.

Yours affectionately

Ivor

My Dear Chapman

Indeed you are darlings of a special sort. The birthday book of my beloved William[1] is charming, and you know what I think of the oatcake and scones you make. But why have you not written in the book? Where are your birthdays? I suppose the dangerous looking tin is a footwarmer? O individuals of great price. As for leave, and consequently coming to see you, I knows nowt. Not before Friday week anyhow, as far as I can see.

So please expect me on a visit either next Saturday or Sunday, but this is not certain. The Band has had some rough times lately, and one hardly knows what is going to happen. But Cheero. Leave cannot be long away; anyway not if the strong rumour is true that we are moving in February. Goodbye everybody.

1. Wordsworth

Dad and the Lad. Mick and the Rest of the Click.

Yours affectionately

Ivor

My Dear Chapman

After all, Harvey could not get leave, and so every part of my plan miscarried, and we never met. Well, well; so wags the world. Receive herewith the grateful wherewithal. This is chiefly to let you know that we are nearly certain to be off on Saturday to Tidworth that haunt of devils. If so, it is not so far from Reading – and – consequently from the Merry Chapmans. Prepare to receive music and books forthwith.

Yous affectionately

Ivor

On 19th February 1916, Gurney's battalion were taken by train to Tidworth, from where they marched through heavy snow to Park House Camp on Salisbury Plain. They arrived to find that there were no beds, fires or electric lights. The men slept on the bare floor through a bitterly cold night of wind and snow.

Pte Gurney
D Co 2/5 Glosters
Park House Camp
Salisbury

My Dear Comtesse

I was sorry to receive so sad a letter from you. One does not like to think of one's friends suffering, and for your complaint, I have of course a particular feeling. I hope that you are not eating too little; that is worse than eating too much by far.

Yes, we have left Chelmsford all right, we did so a fortnight ago; and have been literally freezing ever since. It *has* been cold, and most of us are wheezing and coughing when we are not standing at 'shun or other impossible situations. I might mention, madam, that should you – I say, if you *should* happen to send a parcel of eatables, it would not be wasted. Also, if you could, would you get me another stopper for the air-cushion; the original stopper has got lost, and the poor cushion lies useless in my valise.

I hope all the kids are well and happy, occasionally playing ping-pong as a sort of sacramental remembrance of IBG. And E. Chapman, who will receive the most tremendous licking at chess next time we meet – with P – R4 & Kt to B3, K,B to QB5 etc.

I think we are not very far from going now. A man from the brigade office – who may know nothing says 3 weeks. I just dodder on and worry as little as my mind will let me.

This is a pretty place, far better than we expected, about 3 miles from Tidworth, almost in Hants. And Huts are far away better than tents. There is a stove going all day to toast things by, and make things look more cheerful, and the men are noisy and happy – they are bellowing popular songs, in a robust but sentimental fashion – a good lot of chaps.

Good-bye everybody, and cheer up, ma Comtesse. Always eat a good breakfast, a rule that I live up to now with considerable success. Your description of the concert made me wish a little for music, but not much as yet.

Good bye. Love to everybody.

Yours affectionately

Ivor

Pte Gurney
DCO 2/5 Glosters
Park House Camp
Salisbury

My Dear Chapman

Your parcel was very acceptable to a poor stranded mariner, marooned far from comfortable chairs and hot oatcake and scones; perishing cold, but among men whose cheerfulness not even the devil could daunt, and so, not complaining more than they of my lot.

We don't write many letters here. For myself, I hate the Army so much, and all the worrying little muckings-about fash me so, that I spend the evenings trying to forget all about it. There is firing going on now; I fired the preliminary course, but developed a bad cold, and a catarrh that kept me continually in galvanic movement, no doubt amusing to others, but annoying to myself. But it is merely impossible not to blame oneself in some measure for being unhappy among such men as these. Their vitality is marvellous, their spirits high and continually high.

I am sorry the poor Comtesse has not been well. If good works and a generous heart might make health and happiness, or had I anything to do with the distribution of felicity, she should do very well, but alas! it has little to do with me. I make her a present of our little Regulars back-badge, which we are extremely proud of, are to be allowed to wear, and to me are very pretty. More shall follow when it is possible to obtain them

Thank you kindly for the book which is nearly finished, and then shall be returned, for my book-accommodation is limited, and would do better with you. Thank you very much for the cushion, but is the other one, my name worked thereon, to be wasted for a valve? Nay!

Goodbye, my dears, and bless you all, and again thank you for your cheering letters, like stars in a dark night. Winnie and Micky shall have letters soon. Greeting to the Arch-Power Ted, though he *did* beat me at chess! Yet will I be revenged – revenged.

Yours affectionately

Ivor

POSTCARD (Post mark shows in camp nr. Salisbury)

To: Messrs Chapman, St Michael's, etc.

Message:

Thank you everybody. Letter coming. Meanwhile, please send Davies 'Foliage', and please order R. Bridges Poems in that shilling edition, like the one you keep for me. I think I might set one or two, and must have paper covers. And so, cheero – or Ipsi Pris, as we say.

Ivor

POSTCARD

To: Mrs Chapman, St Michael's, etc.

Message:

I forgot to ask you – will you please send me Davies 'Foliage' – or whatever it's name is – the green covered book. And please send more R.C.M. Magazines to Mr Watson, 46 Juer St, Battersea, London S.W.

My feet – the mud doth stick'em
Would I were at High Wycombe!
In divers muds and mucks
Worse by far than Bucks.

(Unsigned)

To: Mrs Chapman

My Dear Comtesse

Thank you for your letter which shall be replied to when we get to France; and we leave tomorrow night or Wed morning. Here are the cushions. Please get me a valve for the green one, and let me have it some time.

Yours affectionately

Ivor

Love to everybody.

2
FRANCE

May 1916 – September 1917

THE 2ND/5TH GLOSTER REGIMENT SAILED TO LE HAVRE ABOARD A TROOPSHIP ON 25TH MAY 1916 AND MARCHED TOWARDS FLANDERS. FOLLOWING THE LONG MARCH THEY RESTED IN THE VILLAGE OF LE SART, A FEW MILES NORTH OF BETHUNE, BEFORE GOING INTO THE TRENCHES AT RIEZ BAILLEUL FOR A WEEK OF INSTRUCTION UNDER THE LONDON WELSH REGIMENT. THEY RETURNED TO LE SART ON 8TH JUNE AND, TWO DAYS LATER, MOVED INTO A RESERVE POSITION AT LAVENTIE. ON 15TH JUNE THEY MOVED INTO THE FRONT LINE IN THE FAUQUISSART – LAVENTIE SECTOR WHERE THEY REMAINED UNTIL 27TH OCTOBER 1916 WHEN THEY MARCHED SOUTH TO JOIN THE CARNAGE OF THE SOMME OFFENSIVE.

A.F.A. 2042.
114/Gen. No./5248.

FIELD SERVICE
POST CARD

The address only to be written on this side. If anything else is added, the post card will be destroyed.

[Crown Copyright Reserved.]

FIELD POST OFFICE A JU 16 142

Mrs Chapman
St Michaels
Castle Hill
High Wycombe
Bucks England

NOTHING is to be written on this side except the date and signature of the sender. Sentences not required may be erased. If anything else is added the post card will be destroyed.

I am quite well.

~~*I have been admitted into hospital*~~

~~*sick*~~ ~~*and am going on well.*~~
~~*wounded*~~ ~~*and hope to be discharged soon.*~~

~~*I am being sent down to the base.*~~

I have received your *letter dated* ______
~~*telegram*~~ „ ______
~~*parcel*~~ „ ______

Letter follows at first opportunity.

I ~~*have received no letter from you*~~
~~*lately.*~~
~~*for a long time.*~~

Signature only. I B Gurney

Date 13/6/16

[Postage must be prepaid on any letter or post card addressed to the sender of this card.]

(93509) Wt. W3497-293 1,127m. 5/16 J. J. K. & Co., Ltd.

FIELD SERVICE
POST CARD

To: Mrs Chapman, St Michael's, etc.

After deletions, printed message reads:

I am quite well
I have received your letter dated . . .
Letter follows at first opportunity
(Signed) I B Gurney
(date) 13/6/16

First Time In

After the dread tales and red yarns of the Line
Anything might have come to us; but the divine
Afterglow brought us up to a Welsh colony
Hiding in sandbag ditches, whispering consolatory
Soft foreign things. Then we were taken in
To low huts candle-lit, shaded close by slitten
Oilsheets, and there the boys gave us kind welcome,
So that we looked out as from the edge of home,
Sang us Welsh things, and changed all former notions
To human hopeful things. And the next day's guns
Nor any line-pangs ever quite could blot out
That strangely beautiful entry to war's rout;
Candles they gave us, precious and shared over-rations –
Ulysses found little more in his wanderings without doubt.
'David of the White Rock', the 'Slumber Song' so soft, and that
Beautiful tune to which roguish words by Welsh pit boys
Are sung – but never more beautiful than there under the guns' noise.

Whom I greet with best wishes, most particularly Arthur and the Governor who are soon to attain the seldom honour of a birthday. Well, we were not out long before we had been put a Company at a time into the trenches. At least two companies, with two other regiments. And we had a strafe too, which caused a few casualties but not to me. It is charged against me that I did not open a certain letter. As a matter of fact, the cushion was never undone. When I received it I decided that it was too good to use, and better to wait till the other valve arrived, which of course I sent for late. Please do not think I do not read *all* letters, even sentimental and religious. Could you but see the rush for letters here, and the disappointment on the faces of the unsuccessful, you would feel pleased indeed. I would send you souvenirs, shrapnel and such like – but that's all forbidden now.

The news of a present of a watch is good. It will save me languishing in gaol perhaps for being late. The chap I depend on for my horology is nearly as uncertain as myself, and I was thinking of dismissing him soon. It would amuse you to see me trying to talk French, but at any rate I can get what I want without much trouble.

My dear people, all of you, the remembrance of that last stay with you is refreshing to one who sleeps in barns, but there are some consolations. The faces and comradeship of the Welsh Regiment we are now with were worth going far to meet, and they sing their old songs. Picture my joy.

I regret to say that the Army sees to it that one has enough money on leave by dishing out only 5 francs a week to us, and that irregularly. We get also but a quarter loaf of bread, but the French bread is excellent – in great round slabs. Very grateful after the drier Army bread is its dampness and yielding quality. The chocolate is excellent, and the people very kind. It is surprising to see everything as usual very well within reach of the guns. They used to shell the villages but do not seem to now. There is quite a fine church a few yards from me shattered but still noble, and under the shadow of it the estaminets are doing good trade – maybe with windows shattered, the children play; and the country a mile or so behind the firing line is green and peaceful as our Dear England's.

A bon sante of all, but more especially of Messieurs Arthur and Le Pere.

Yours affectionately

Ivor

P.S. For goodness sake do not wait till you get my address – this would not be till 'après le guerre'; may be a long time yet.

And you will be pleased to hear that we get letters pretty regularly, in or out of the trenches.

My Dear Comtesse

You are as kind as ever, and your scones as good. It was delightful to get them, and they were eaten with great rejoicing in a little (signallers) barn at the back of a farm in Northern France – somewhere. But – may I say so? – While we are on reserve; in the villages, we can get everything almost we can afford. Tobacco is *much* cheaper than in England. The war taxes do not apply in Army canteens. Those cigarettes, which may have cost you 8d, would cost 4d here. Soap and Cold Cream about the same price as with you. And then there is the enormous postage! We buy French bread – excellent stuff, and cakes. And chocolate is cheaper than the English. It is not nice to say so, but it is better to make presents of food in *money*. The more so as we get the benefit of the exchange. This is bad to say, but everybody out here agrees. The more so as they pay us 5 francs only, instead of 10 as in England. Bread is all we are short of – the A S C steal it – out of the trenches that is easy. *And we are not allowed to carry extra stuff outside haversacks* and in those there is no room.

Well, what of the Russian news? All the puling pessimists and the toadies of Germany swept away by one fact – that the

The church at Laventie, 1916.

Russians got through in 9 hours at one place. This is great – glorious. We will no longer think by rule and measure a la Garvin, but according to our faith – freely and with courage.

The two souvenirs I send were picked up in a ruined bank next to a ruined convent here in this town – where we live in comparative peace so short a distance behind the firing line.

I hope the kids will like them. Arthur and Winnie will make best use of them I think.

I am glad about Kitty, and believe the life will suit her. She has company and some definite interesting new work to do; and what colossal sum the 2/5 would give for that happy fate. God only knows. The motto of the British Army is 'Fed up, but carrying on'. Winnie must be proud she is so much in request. She is the kind of lady who will some day make herself useful if not indispensable in all sorts of ways.

Micky is at present une chere petite diable (femine in this case) and unforgettable in any case. By the way I have already written you a letter. I hope you got it? I know that one letter has reached its destination HEAVILY CENSORED, so that the official eye is On Me.

The Katharine Tynan verses are perfectly charming in that War Poetry cutting. Sweet, original and truly felt. The rest – n'importe. I did not read the slip on Women's influence on Men. Il est vieux jeu. Arthur is making scores of C.B. Fry size now I hope. He will make a good bat, but don't let him tear himself to pieces as a bowler, and share time in the slips as a fielder. *Don't* forget. The news about Mr Rushby Smith is astonishing but I bear up.[1] Go and do thou likewise.

Now I go for half an hour to a cafe where French may be painfully learnt at the cost of two cups – charming people.

Goodbye everybody.

Many happy returns and may I be there to share the next.

Yours affection.

Ivor

Congrats to the Gov: and Arthur

1. The Rev Rushby-Smith was appointed Canon of Oxford

Laventie

One would remember still
Meadows and low hill
Laventie was, as to the line and elm row
Growing through green strength wounded, as home elms grow.
Shimmer of summer there and blue autumn mists
Seen from trench-ditch winding in mazy twists.
The Australian gunners in close flowery hiding
Cunning found out at last, and smashed in the unspeakable lists.
And the guns in the smashed wood thumping and grinding.
The letters written there, and received there,
Books, cakes, cigarettes in a parish of famine,
And leaks in rainy times with general all-damning.
The crater, and carrying of gas cylinders on two sticks
(Pain past comparison and far past right agony gone),
Strained hopelessly of heart and frame at first fix.

Café-au-lait in dug-outs on Tommies' cookers,
Cursed minniewerfs, thirst in eighteen-hour summer.
The Australian miners clayed, and the being afraid
Before strafes, sultry August dusk time than death dumber –
And the cooler hush after the strafe, and the long night of wait –
The relief of first dawn, the crawling out to look at it,
Wonder divine of dawn, man hesitating before Heaven's gate.
(Though not on Cooper's where music fire took at it.
Though not as at Framilode beauty where body did shake at it)
Yet the dawn with aeroplanes crawling high at Heaven's gate
Lovely aerial beetles of wonderful scintillate
Strangest interest, and puffs of soft purest white –
Seeking light, dispersing colouring for fancy's delight.
Of Machonachie, Paxton, Tickler and Gloucester's Stephens;
Fray Bentos, Spiller and Baker, odds and evens
Of trench food, but the everlasting clean craving
For bread, the pure thing, blessèd beyond saving.
Canteen disappointments, and the keen boy braving
Bullets or such for grouse roused surprisingly through
(Halfway) Stand-to.

And the shell nearly blunted my razor at shaving;
Tilleloy, Fauquissart, Neuve Chapelle, and mud like glue.
But Laventie, most of all, I think is to soldiers
The town itself with plane trees, and small-spa air;
And vin, rouge-blanc, chocolat, citron, grenadine:
One might buy in small delectable cafés there.
The broken church, and vegetable fields bare;
Neat French market-town look so clean,
And the clarity, amiability of North French air.

Like water flowing beneath the dark plough and high Heaven,
Music's delight to please the poet pack-marching there.

My *Dear Old Winnie*

Thank you for your jolly letter which I enjoyed very much, with all its bits of news and gossip. Bon. And I am glad to hear about Kitty's great success in her new sphere of existence.

And, from my influential friend the Comtesse de Tilda how Arthur is getting on at le cricket. Bless his little heart. Stap me, but tis a sprightly youth. Also it pleases me that you are so much in request as a vocalist. My dear kid, continue you in the straight and narrow way, take as pattern the high example set you by my good friends the Rushby-Smith girls and it will give me the greatest pleasure, apres le guerre to confer on you the famous order of the Icy Glare.

I suppose Ping Pong is still impossible for you. Alas this is a horrible war. And they don't give us enough bread in it, confound 'em. He asked for bread and they gave him a stony look. Oliver Twist would have a bad time out here I fear. How is your frail body, too weak to bear all the strain as yet your spirit would put upon it? Anyway go on steadily: some day it will stand a lot. My jaws for instance have developed terrific crushing powers, absolutely unimaginable to the ordinary low down civilian.

Arthur and Micky shall have letters very soon, and but for the fact that another letter is overdue and these will go off tonight, they should have them now. Meanwhile, cheer up my estimable female, and hope for the end of the war which chiefly bores me. Though two nights ago it was sufficiently exciting. There is difficulty in showing where we are placed but opposite Lille will do maybe. Micky shall not have to wait long for a letter from Laventie as we are in reserve for a time. Good bye mes chers enfants. Expect me to tea on Sunday.

Yours affectionately

Ivor

(Field Post Office date stamp on envelope: JY 27 16)

My Dear Count

(that is if you *do* count) I snatch a peaceful hour at 1 a.m. to assure you that those cigars were far better than anything I could have made from your parcel-wrappings. Indeed, I will go so far as to say that they tasted as if they had been really bought at a shop, had it not been war-time, and if homemade, do (or did) you great credit. They tell me you have taken up Bowls, which seems to show that you recognise your status and disabilities at last, and will soon be content to yield up the reins into your son's hands – a promising youth of considerable military reputation.

You have not submitted any further names of offers of appointments to my judgement, so suppose that there are no further offers. Or is it that there are too many?

Well, well, I will not condemn unheard.

Things are moving out here as you may have heard lately. Do you happen to know whether our Nobs consider the thing satisfactory? I thought you might have gathered some notion. War don't suit me, sir, and I don't care who knows it, unless the Kaiser gets trying any of his tricks. And to hide in holes from flying whizzbangs and gradually to approach the state of

The trenches at Laventie.

An old gun position in Sanctuary Wood, in the Ypres sector, 25/10/17.

Battle of Arras, April 1917, machine gun post in captured trench.

doddering grandmotherliness is not my idea of Fun. But here's the job ready to my hand, and what must be done, shall be done. Though selling chip potatoes in Hell seems to us occasionally to have merits superior to this life.

Well, someday I may return to a life with kids in it, and flowers and a real white tablecloth, and more cigars. Meanwhile Cheero, my giddy Goods Manager.

Yours affectionately

Ivor

(Headed: Addresses in future only Name, Co, reg: and B E F France)

My *Dear Old Winnie,*

Still a war on! and I still in it! How I envy Kitty, and her rise in wages! It is really an achievement though to have stuck at hard work and got a rise. And I congratulate her very much. Cheero!

You must hurry up and get strong and fit and well: do stunts on the parallel bars, and lift dumbells by nervous convulsion only. On such meagre routine do the great thrive. Dear kid; it is a different sort of life now to the December of two years ago. Ping pong between the lines has been stopped, and I no longer play accompaniments for the Germans. Soon they will stop us inviting each other to tea. The German spy system is excellent. Wonderful! They manage to find out when any oatcake arrives for me, and if I do not ask them over, invariably said before they think it all gone, I will spend the last drop of my blood to defend the last crumb of La Comtesse's oatmeal.

I thought of you on All Hallows eve, (Hallowmas Eve, isn't it?) and imagined you performing some strange Gaelic rites of memory and sanctification. I hope you had 'Sweet Polly Oliver' or the 'Bay of Biscay' in memory of one not yet needing rites but only remembrance.

The soap I am using now, but not the baccy. The oatcake had but a short life, but an appreciated one. Goodbye and Love to everybody.

Your affectionate friend

Ivor

My Dear Old Win

Still here and not there, as is perhaps to be expected. No leave yet, that is to say; but who knows? I may arrive home from the office tonight and find a telegram 'Will you come and teach me how? Lloyd George' (reply half-prepaid). Or 'Do stop them, old man – Wilhelm' (not pre-paid) lying on the hall table. This might mean quite a few days in Blighty, in which case I shall hurry at once to St Micks (Collis castelli – Castle Hill) and present my never-for-one-single-phsycological [sic]-moment-to-be-forgotten Winifred with the one souvenir I have – the tattered remains of a G. pocket book – if it lasts till then.

I hope Christmas went off all right and fine – that Daddy was not grumpy and La Comtesse grumpy at his grumpiness. I trust you danced the roundelay and Fa-la-la-ed to any extent. Stap me, had I been there, would not I have taken part in these innocent revels? Yea, by the to [sic] old Pig of Brixham, marry, so would I!

And how's Arthur and how's that little imp of restlessness Micky, the human Soap-Bubble? How many goals has Arthur the Hope of his Side managed to score?

I want to know all Mrs. It is port wine oatcakes and chews of bacca to me. Hogmanay was happy and rowdy just round here – happier than it was in Scotland the men come back from leave say.

Well I hope High Wycombe put some go into the parting kick.

Good bye

Yours affectionately

Ivor

In February 1917 Gurney's battalion moved to the Ablaincourt Sector and followed the German strategic withdrawal eastward from village to village. At Caulaincourt two companies of the Gloucesters, including Gurney's, sheltered in the still-standing mausoleum. On 31st March the battalion reached Vermand. On Good Friday night Gurney was wounded in the arm and had to be sent to hospital in Rouen, where he remained for six weeks.

At the end of May 1917 Gurney was transferred to a Machine-Gun company and given a new Service number (241281) but remained attached to the 2nd/5th Glosters who were now at the Arras front.

POSTCARD addressed to: Winnie, St. Michael's, etc.
View of ROUEN.

No Message.

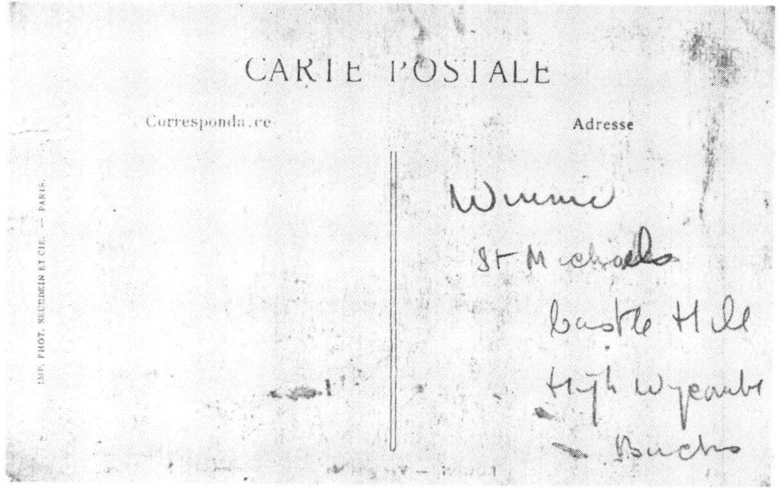

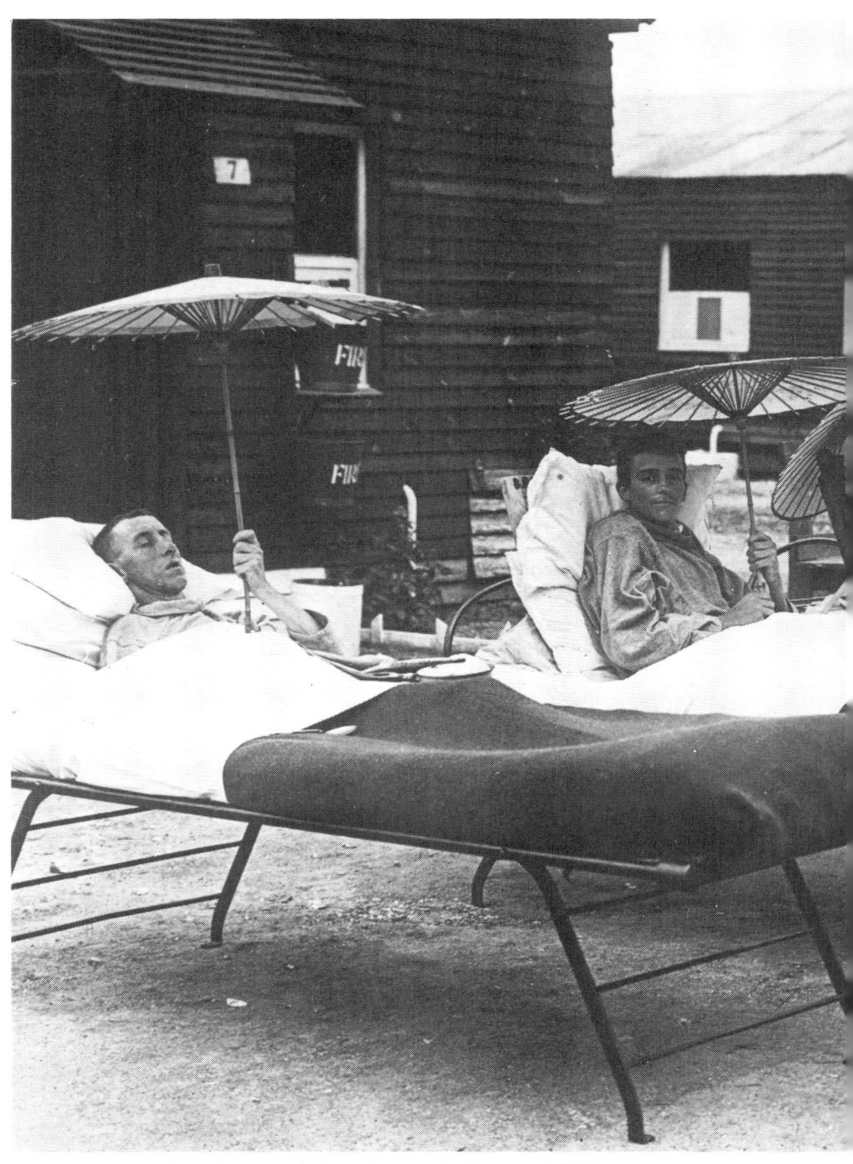

British wounded in hospital, Rouen 1/6/17.

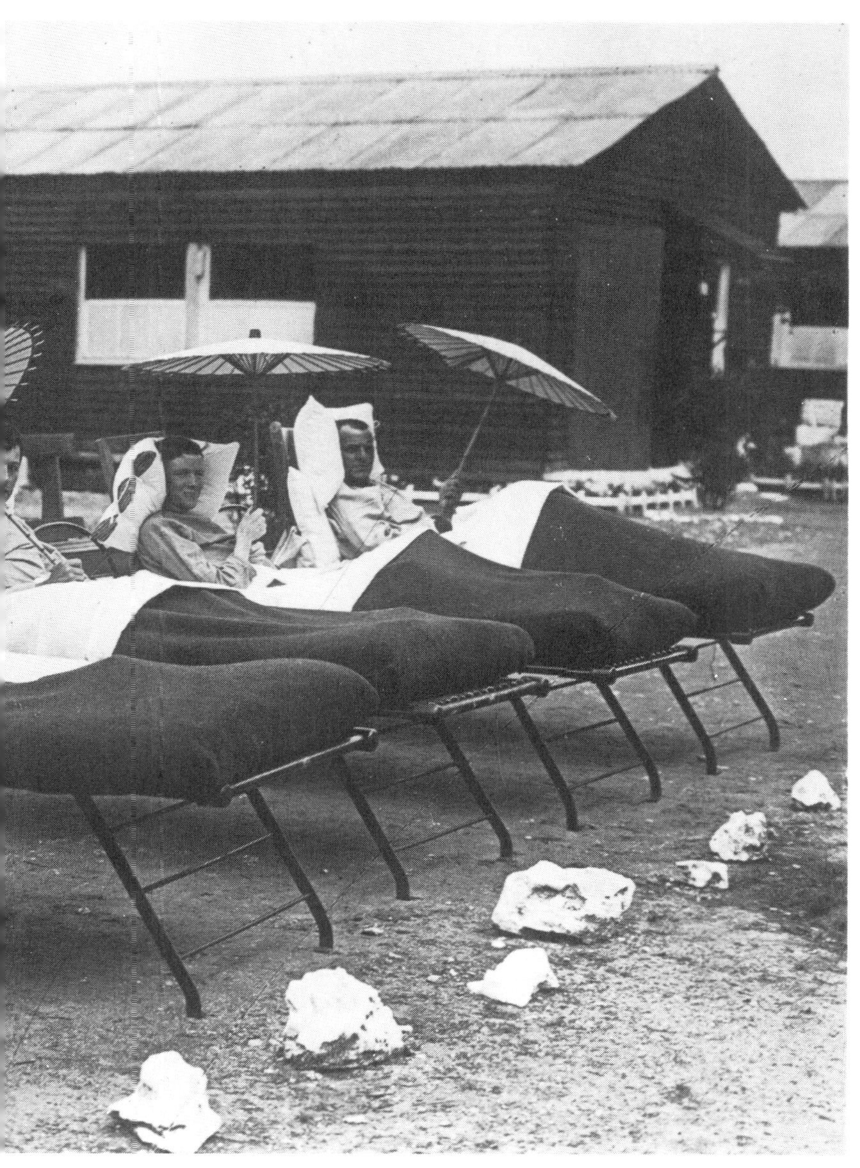

Remains of a line of German strong points near St. Julien, 12/10/17.

My Dear Winnie

I hope you have received the cards I sent a few days ago, and like them. Also that you poor creatures are not absolutely starving in poor old Blighty. They will soon prohibit the sending of cakes out here, and about time if all tales are true; you must be a nest of walking skeletons.

Are you all pretty well, now? The weather is certainly not cold, anyway, and you can get out. Do you play games ever? How is the Comtesse, worker of miracles out of oatmeal and plain flour? and Daddy with his weight of natural cares? How is Arthur doing at cricket? As for Mick, I never could believe her sick till the mourning cards were issued, and she is probably as naughty (and nice) as ever.

They are chucking us out at any time now – Hup the line: Hover the top and the best of luck. Tuesday must see us off I think, so please write to the Batt: in future. The next wound I have will bring me more luck, or else I shall have cutting remarks to make to the Lord Almighty. How are the Christ Church people – His special delegates and assistants. And how is the Pet Lootenant[1] doing in France?

I have lost your mascot that you put in my overcoat. It had stayed there carefully cherished until Good Friday Night when we went over, and since then – well I shall be lucky if I see ever a thing again.

What must the High Wycombe hills look like now! Great clouds of miraculous green, green that looks alive and gifted with a voice.

Here endeth the last letter from the Base.

Yours affectionately

Ivor

1. Lt. Wildsmyth

Towards Lillers

In October marching, taking the sweet air,
Packs riding lightly, and homethoughts soft coming,
'This is right marching, we are even glad to be here,
Or very glad?' But looking upward to dark smoke foaming,
Chimneys on the clear crest, no more shades for roaming,
Smoke covering sooty what man's heart holds dear,
Lillers we approached, a quench for thirsty frames,
And looked once more between houses and at queer names
Of estaminets, longed for cool wine or cold beer.
This was war; we understood; moving and shifting about;
To stand or be withstood in the mixèd rout
Of fight to come after this. But that was a good dream
Of justice or strength-test with steel tool a gleam
Made to the hand. But barb-wire lay to the front,
Tiny aeroplanes circled as ever their wont
High over the two ditches of heart-sick men;
The times scientific, as evil as ever again.
October lovely bathing with sweet air the plain.

Gone outward to the east and the new skies
Are aeroplanes, and flat there as tiny as bright
As insects wonderful coloured after the night
Emerging lovely as ever into the new day's
First coolness and lucent gratefulness
Of the absorbing wide prayer of middle sight.
Men clear their rifles insentient at that delight;
Wonder increases as the night dies.

Now up to the high above aeroplanes go
swift bitter smoke puffs and spiteful flames,
None knows the pilots, none guesses at their names,
They fly unthought courses of common danger,
Honour rides on the frame with them through that anger,
As the heroes of Marathon their renown we know.

Kitty (at right) with two Land Army friends, 1916.

My Dear Mr C.

Nothing, as your acute intellect will perceive, has yet happened to me. I am still all in one piece, but a bored, humiliated, altogether fed up piece of humanity, who looks for the end of the war to deliver him from bondage. And just as I reach this, it turns out that a German aeroplane is soaring over us, and so our anti-aircraft guns are potting and sending lovely little white fleeces of cloud high up against a quite perfect blue. But Fritz when he attempts these daring feats takes good care to fly as near Heaven as he will ever get, whereas our men fly low and saunter along – a cheering sight.

When you write, as I hope you will, please send me some facts about munitions. As how a piece of waste land, chiefly distinguished for its fine vein of sardine and pineapple tins, has now been turned into the most amazing group of works turning out by thousands of tons a day shells of the most remarkable destructivity. Any little facts like this, or the Rev Horatio Bottomley's prediction of the close of hostilities in June before last; anything like this will bring a smile to the wasted lips of a soldier. But don't breathe a word of anything nasty happening after the end of August or else you will run the risk of extreme unpopularity with the gallant defenders of your country.

I hear that you are frightfully busy and so out of mischief. What would I not give for the chance of good clean honest work, instead of the aimless mucking-about! I envy Kitty[1] with all my heart, so do all we. She seems to have done very well, and to be 'busy, well, and jolly . . .' Oh squirms from the Gallery! Almost two years ago I was driving a tedding machine with the Severn, May Hill, Malverns and Cotswolds to look at. But all these joys have descended upon the women, who seem quite capable of doing the job. I wish they would tackle this one. No. 3895 is always ready to resign. With best wishes

Yours affectionately

Ivor Gurney

1. Kitty was in the Land Army

Micky

June 22

My Dear Comtesse

No present could have given me more pleasure than this one. The very best, and 'twill no doubt save me much trouble. We have just come out of trenches after a strafe that a man who had been through Loos described as being worse than Loos while it lasted. Well, it is as well to do the thing properly. I am glad to be out of it, glad to have been through it, and the Glosters are a good crowd, bless 'em. But it seems doubtful whether I should ever see High Wycombe again. I think 6 inches or so lower would have given much opportunity for damage to 10 high explosives, which burst about 30 yards behind us. I had my eye, or part of it round the corner of the bay, and it was a fine sight. Also I was as cool as now, writing this letter. This suits me, but it don't put my belly right, or make me less introspective, confound it! All I wished for was to play the G minor Prelude from Part II – Bach, when it was all over. But there was only more brick biscuits to chaw. I hope my generous benefactress you are pretty well and kicking fairly strongly. I hope for a nice blighty to come and see you all before long.

Yours affectionately

Ivor Gurney

My Dear Comtesse

(Whack! there goes another mosquito!)

It was delightful to get your letter tonight, and to renew my acquaintance with pleasant memories.

I am glad that Kitty seems to have dropped into her proper place, and in a nice direction too. Syde is quite unknown to me, however. Daddy I hope is as expert at bowls as at Chess, though if he has been boasting, I withdraw all that. He sent some good cigars though. It was all of a good parcel that. The oatcake was a Creation, an inspiration of high degree. The cake was good enough, and the tallow candles of a taste the most delectable. Cigars too, thought I. Buck ye up! thought I! Wha's the warl' comin' tae? (I believe that may pass). Luckily it got to me in the trenches, and so there was no need either to carry it, or eat it hastily. Also, we have been out of civilisation so much that I am quite wealthy – for me. In trenches one cannot buy, and then parcels are as manna of the best make.

What a pity it was you missed the songs. I knew myself very late, but thought the letter might just scrape home in time to give you notice. There nearly was a disaster about the singer, but not quite – thanks to H.N.H. and Miss Scott, who hung on like valiant limpets.[1]

But how can one concentrate one's mind on higher affairs when these beastly mosquito's are gradually biting one to a shadow? It's no possible wumman. But thank you for your letter. My intellects wanted something restful and homey, and your letter supplied the want. St Thomas a Kempis is a ruddy unmitigated bore. I am afraid High Wycombe will receive some bad news soon from this way. If you send me a book ever, let it be small. I ask no more, so low and humble have my desires become. Pity the poor egotist!

Love to everybody.

Yours affectionately

Ivor

1. Herbert Howells and Marion Scott arranged for two of Gurney's songs, composed in the trenches, to be performed at the Royal College of Music in July 1917. They were settings of John Masefield's 'By a Bierside' and F.W. Harvey's 'In Flanders'.

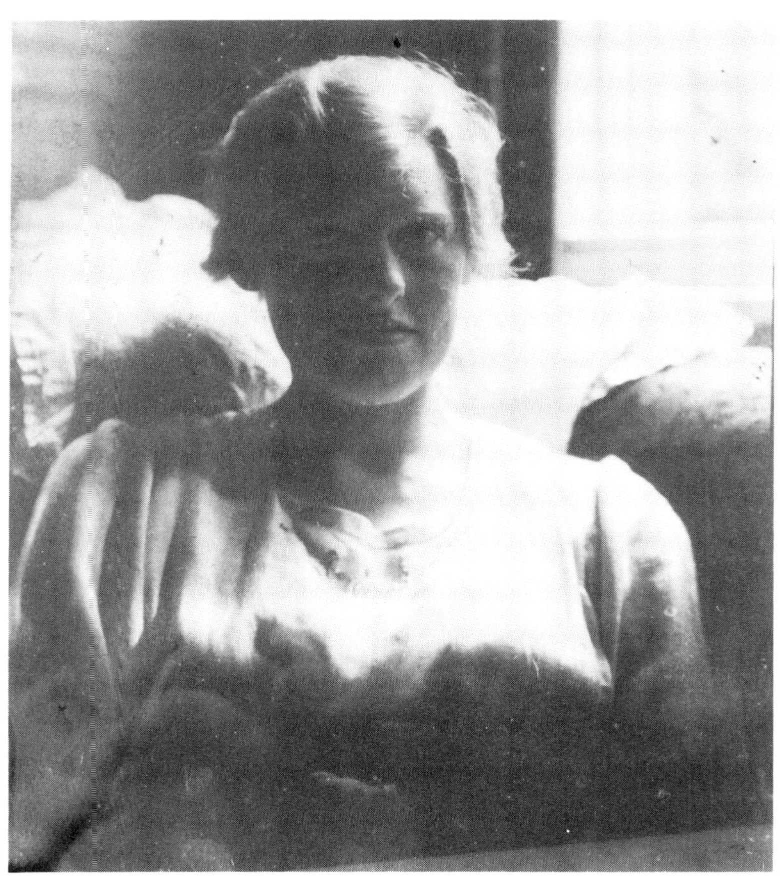

Kitty

Arthur

My Dear Arthur

Go you on and prosper, and rise from the 'not out 0' to the 'not out 20'. Then from 'not out 0' 1st eleven to undreamed of heights. It only means coolness with you, who have all the other gifts, necessary for big scores. You should have bits of shrapnel and so on, if it were allowed to send them, but the official foot is hard down on such little presents. Lying in my dugout or funkhole the other day, I became too bored to read serious stuff, or write letters; so turning my attention to the few filthy magazines strewn around, left by the last visitants, I became aware of a thrilling boys tale of 3 scouts who apparently played the very deuce and all with the Germans. It was so absolutely unlike the real thing that I read quite a lot of it, and laughed a great deal. At present it is chiefly – sticking it; with the prospect of a big bust soon. Machine guns all going at once are the terrifying things, and I don't like 'em.

Everything goes well with you I hope. You've got brains enough to do the lessons they will give you, if you take it coolly and don't worry. The only way I can clean equipment and rifle (and O how I hate doing that silly old job over and over again) is to do the first thing – any 'first thing', and let the rest sort itself out.

Here is a song our men sang when the last strafe was at its hottest – a very popular song about here; but not military.

I want to go home, I want to go home
The whizzbangs and shrapnel they whistle and roar.
I don't want to go in the trenches no more,
Take me over the sea
Where the Alleman can't catch me.
O my! I don't want to die.
I want to go home.

Not a brave song, but brave men sing it.

Yours affectionately

Ivor

Winnie and Micky

My Dear Old Winnie

Bless you my child; yours was a nice letter for a war weary son of a gun to get.

I hope you will get your reward at Perran, and play endless exciting games of tennis; and have delightful cool – but not chilly – bathes, generally enjoying yourself as you deserve.

Well, it doesn't look much like seeing you for some ages yet. Before this week 1 man a company per week was *supposed* to go. This week leave is again violently smitten on the head (a frequent occurrence with us) and may have succumbed to its injuries.

My fairy-godmother is most frightfully slack. Perhaps she is after the vote on Proportional Representation or summat new-fangled. I am, I hope I may say – a just man, a long-suffering and humble servant; (Don't this sound like Lloyd George) but even fairy god-mothers can get it in the neck. And this particular one has been asking for it for a pretty long time.

When will the days of peace and plenty and beaucoup ping pong once again return? Alack, man knoweth not. Nor young women either, in spite of their growing up, putting their hair up, putting on frills, and fine raiment, and generally startling and upsetting their humble adorers – of whom

I am

(Very affectionately)

one of the wormiest and most enthralled

Ivor

My Dear Winnie

I did not write on your birthday. Too many things cropped up for that. But it was remembered; the first since Arthur's that is set down in the book your revered Pa bestowed upon me. And now you are down at Perranporth, listening to the sea. Possibly bathing in it. 'Fore Jove, a lucky wench! No bathe for me this lovely morning but a dip in an old biscuit tin – such terrible hardships do war heroes undergo. But don't let this disturb you. Please enjoy yourself double for both of our sakes. And let the others follow your excellent example. Let your sand castles outdo the windiest vapourings of Sir Walter Scott, and your mud-pies outdo those of the Ritz or Carlton.

And tell me how the rabbits get on, and if they are still cannibalistic in their nasty habits, which is distressing.

In my next letter, which will be to Micky, there will be found a collection of be-yutiful drawings or stupendous epics; I have not yet decided which. However it is for me much easier to say 'The cow stands on four legs' than to depict the animal caught in the act. I can do the four legs with tolerable success. It is planting the cow on top of them that bothers me. The man who invented cows was a clever chap, and should be heartily congratulated by the Affiliated Society of Cunning Milkmen. Ping pong is more na pooh than ever I suppose. But wouldn't a hard wet sand table look well with little celluloid balls dancing about it? I wish I were with you to experiment, and to run races on the sand or to take down Arthur's pride at le criquette.

Yours affectionately

Ivor

3
BLIGHTY

IN AUGUST 1917 THE GLOSTERS MOVED NORTH TO THE YPRES FRONT. BY EARLY SEPTEMBER THEY WERE IN ST. JULIEN FACING THE PASSCHENDAELE RIDGE. IVOR GURNEY WAS GASSED.

In September 1917 Gurney was evacuated from France to the Bangour War Hospital, near Edinburgh. Whilst there he fell in love with one of his nurses, Annie Nelson Drummond. In October *Severn and Somme* was published. However, Gurney was not content: he found it difficult to adjust to the quiet hospital life, considered himself a 'wangler' but dreaded the return to the trenches which full recovery threatened. By early November he was fit enough to leave hospital but, due to a stomach upset ('presumably due to gas; wink, wink!'),[1] he was not sent back to France straight away. Instead, after a few days' leave spent with the Chapmans in High Wycombe and at home in Gloucester, he was posted to a signalling course at the Command Depot, Seaton Delaval, Northumberland.

After he left Bangour, Gurney and Miss Drummond continued to correspond and his hopes of a happy future with her grew. Only in letters to his dear friend Herbert Howells did he confide his true feelings about Miss Drummond: 'O Erbert, O Erbert . . . I forgot my body walking with her; a thing that has not happened since . . . when? I really don't know'.

Gurney found the camp at Seaton Delaval a 'freezing, ugly, uncomfortable Hell of a Hole'.[2] Life there was cold and meaningless to him; there was no comradeship comparable with that which, in adversity, he had enjoyed in France, and which had inspired him then. Very soon the enemy 'neurasthenia' began to haunt him once more, as it had before 1914. In February 1918 he was returned to hospital in Newcastle-upon-Tyne, and from there to Brancepeth Castle, County Durham. For a while his symptoms seem to have subsided and on 12th March he wrote to Herbert Howells from Brancepeth: 'I am happy today with a letter from A.N.D. after another both charming, so shake hands; and her presence is strong on me as I write'. He was able to compose again; then, in late March, he wrote to Marion Scott: 'Yesterday I felt and talked to (I am serious) the spirit of Beethoven'. Although he felt a spiritual uplifting through this experience he knew that a more sinister interpretation could be put upon it. He

1. Letter to Marion Scott, 3 November 1917.
2. Letter to Marion Scott, January 1918.

ends: 'This letter is quite sane, n'est ce pas?' By May his mental condition had worsened and he was sent to Lord Derby's War Hospital at Warrington for treatment of a 'nervous breakdown'. At about this time, Annie Drummond severed her correspondence with Gurney and his mind turned to black despair.

On 19th June he wrote a good-bye letter to Marion Scott: 'I know you would rather know me dead than mad'. He was found by the canal at Warrington but the courage to end his life failed him. Comradeship, love and hope – all had deserted him.

On 4th July he was transferred to the Middlesex War Hospital at Napsbury, and there he remained until his discharge from the Army in October 1918 with a pension of twelve shillings per week. The war ended in November.

B2 The Camp
Bangour
near Edinburgh

My Dear Winnie

Here's t'ye, my bonnie lass, and don't you forget it. Soon the fatal chuckout will come and before going out I be granted a golden holiday from the Army. On which happy occasion you are to behold me once again, a gallant sojer with a loathing of everything in the whole bangshoot except the men chiefly oppressed.

Fair and charming damsel, once again will I present my respects to you, and tell you All about Myself, and walk up Keep Hill, and read and douse the glim late, and stick my feet on the mantlepiece in disreputable old slippers, and smoke a guggly churchwarden, and bless you my child, and wish I was a fixture for a while, and tootle the freudlich Bach and the triste Chopin, and frowst, and behave myself as though I were in a properly-conducted family of high ethical status.

I wonder whether I shall do all this? Je ne sais pas; anyway I will cherish the Chapman family in my bosom and criticise Haig's strategy as though I knew all about it.

Yours affectionately

Ivor

O yes, and you can say something every now and then.

My Dear Winnie

Here is a book I thought you would like; I hope you won't mind the markings: they are simply what pleased me. Dear old kid it was nice to see you, and nicer to see you again. At present, or at least on Monday I am to be put on a signalling course to last from 2 to 4 months; time to think of a commission after that, old girl.

The copies of my book have not yet come, and I can't afford to buy any more. Directly it comes you shall have one. The papers have been kind to it – especially Times and Morning Post. Did you take away the photo of yourself from the set I had? If so, you lay yourself open to extreme penalties, and utmost rigour of the law.

This place is a pit village, ugly enough but the (rather tame) sea is only 4 miles away, and the wind roars continually. This is the address.

Pte Gurney 241281
C Coy, 4th Reserve Batt:
Gloucesters
Seaton Delaval
Northumberland

Has Kitty got a new post yet? I hope she will get as good a one as she deserves. I hope everybody is well, Mammy, Daddy and the brats Arthur and Micky, who has such a persuasive tongue.

Goodbye best wishes to you and everybody

Yours affectionately

Ivor

(Written at head of letter) Paper and String not to hand. Book comes when they come.

My *Dear Winnie*

Here is a tiny note for you which may get to you by Xmas Day, or long before, or long after, as the case may be. Anyway enjoy it – my dear enemy (at ping pong). Alas! I know not if the sport of ping-pong still flourishes anywhere in the land.

Lately, I have shirked much on account of a disturbed interior. RAMC, Rest Station, and now on a job – a comparatively nice one to do with water-carts. This is all very well, but I have had no letters. Please write to me. Private

Gurney 2/5 Glos. attached Sanitary Section 61st Div HQ. That will reach me I think.

I wonder how you have been lately with all this grey unpleasant weather. No bon! no bon!

And Arthur and Mick both of whom shall receive the polished epistle. Cheero!

There will be no long walk for us this Xmas – but there is a good chance of leave soon, and then who knows what wonders will happen?

Yes, Leave. When? Don't know, but a good leave – no skimpy allowance of a day.

My dear kids there will be joy then and much galumphing, even though they may be meatless days, and only 3 courses. Does the New Vicaw appreciate Mrs Chapman's excellent scones? I hope he has not taken my place – in the slippers only large enough because of the holes. Don't let him have any oatcakes. I have heard and met so many Scots lately on this Job, that I have tasted oatcake quite often in fancy lately. O to do so in reality.

Bon O Bon

Yours affect.

Ivor

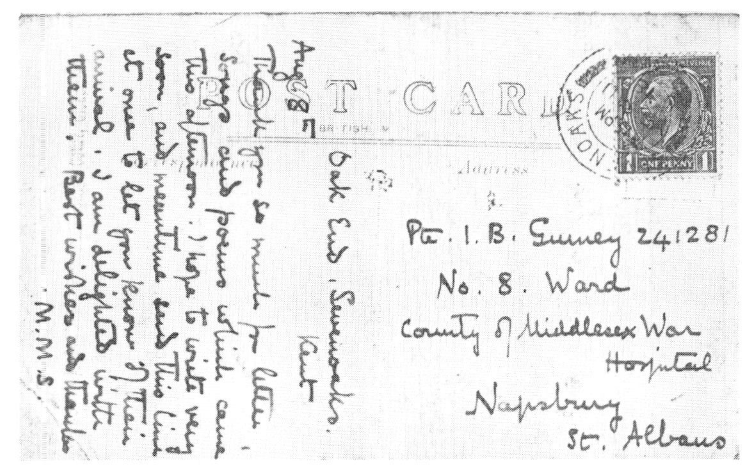

POST CARD

From: Marion Scott

To: Pte I.B. Gurney 241281,
No. 8 Ward
County of Middlesex
War Hospital, etc.

August 8th.

Thank you so much for letter, songs and poems which came this afternoon. I hope to write very soon, and meantime send this line at once to let you know of their arrival. I am delighted with them. Best wishes and thanks
(Signed) M.M.S.

Turmut Hoeing

I straightened my back from turmut-hoeing
And saw, with suddenly opened eyes,
Tall trees, a meadow ripe for mowing,
And azure June's cloud-circled skies.

Below, the earth was beautiful
Of touch and colour, fair each weed,
But Heaven's high beauty held me still,
Only of music had I need.

And the white-clad girl at the old farm,
Who smiled and looked across at me,
Dumb was held by that strong charm
Of cloud-ships sailing a foamless sea.

No 8 Ward
Middlesex War Hospital
Napsbury

My Dear Winnie

There's 10 minutes or so to pass before breakfast, and you shall have the benefit thereof. The Most Gracious Comtesse has received a letter from me lately I believe (my head's like a colander, and cannot hold much) but if this is not so she shall receive fullest consideration or notification of the same.

I wonder whether you are more stately than once you were, and what new accomplishments have come to you in the past year – whether you can make Simnel Cakes or burnish halberds or starch ruffs; or pickle peppercorns or any of a hundred useful things to be known by the young of that species, woman. My (?) there's a whole world of accomplishments that has come to me here. Polishing floors, rubbing brasses, washing pots, pans, kettles, floors; hoeing mangels and turmuts! ('Give I the turmut hoeing'). You see this is a new list – in which piano playing does not appear – for though the spirit is willing, the flesh is weak enough to quail before the looks of some folk here when they look up from cards or snoozing with a look either of amazed contempt or bitter anger! Well, well, there is always something to put up with in this crocky old world of tears. But of this I hope there is no trace at Perran. Don't get 'flu' or any other silly old disease. What do you do with your time – is it cricket, sand castles or mud pies? Would that this poor mortal were with you dashing about, and finding out the colour of sea water from the depth of a yard.

Comme ca, m'selle! Observe the dash from a height – the slow float and the gradual return!! A masterpiece, without doubt. I hope soon to be in a position to do such mad delightful things, and then great works without number (Symphony No 8 dedicated to Winifred Chapman) will simply leak from my pen. Arthur shall have a special portrait in music, of his making a century at full speed with beaucoup boundaries. Until then, ma chère mamselle I suscribe [sic] myself, with love

Yours affectionately

Ivor

Pte Gurney 241281
C Coy 4th Res: Batt:
Gloucesters

My Dear Winnie

That blooming book has got stolen, I suppose, for no memory of sending it to you do I remember.

It was, poor thing, *The Old Country*, a YMCA book, which had some good stuff. Still, here's one of the most lovely little books I know.

'The Old Bed' is simply perfect.

The first five Sonnets very good.

'I saw three pigs a riding', 'Tenants' and some more first rate. This is very precious to me, Wilfred Gibson is a master.

Sorry you haven't had my book yet. S and Js are slow.

The Times, *Morning Post* and *Telegraph* have liked it. With love to you all.

Yours affectionately

Ivor Gurney

Where's that photograph? What! What!

19 Barton St
Gloucester

My Dear Winnie

I hope you will like this book: it seems to me to be one of the jolliest and best packed books going.

Charles Doughty, Barrie, Housman (A E), Dr. John Brown, G K C, Lucas, Sorley, Ledwidge, R. Bridges – let me especially recommend. I do hope all you lovely people will have a good time at High Wycombe since there are none better deserve it; and O that I were along to share it with you, you dear children and grown ups! Alas there'll be no I.B.G. to smoke his churchwarden and deliver weighty sentences after the style of Dr Johnson. Someday, and soon, (for I am to return to College) St Mike's will shelter me once again, and O will there be ping-pong? Will the state of Europe permit frivolities, think you? Let's hope there will be a great flurry of snow that night to encircle the feasting house with white wonder untouched till Micky goes out to dance on it. That night Miss Marjory shall play Beethoven's most difficult Sonata and Arthur wriggle his eeliest. The fond parents looking on indulgently the while, bless 'em, for in calibre precision of fire and general aptitude for service they are level with the best. My best respex to you all and may you like this presink.

Yours affectionately

Ivor Gurney

4
POSTSCRIPT

Following his release from the Army Gurney returned to his parents' home in Gloucester. His father was terminally ill and his mother pre-occupied. He met with resentment from his brother, Ronald, who probably considered Ivor's long hospitalisation to have been contrived to avoid further active service. Ronald cannot have understood the very real distress which Gurney was suffering, plagued as he was by imagined voices in the head and by an inability to control his hopelessly irregular eating habits.

Finding little affinity with his family at home, Gurney seriously considered going away to sea. Within a few days of his arrival home he went to Lydney in an effort to find a ship. Having no luck there he walked overnight the twenty-three miles to Newport but again found no ship to take him. He borrowed money and, the next day, returned to Gloucester, arriving back at lunchtime. That same afternoon Mr Chapman arrived from High Wycombe to see Gurney and was saddened to learn of his condition. There was a long discussion with the family, during which Mr Chapman offered to adopt Ivor; this proposal was not accepted by the proud Gurneys. However, Mr Chapman was at least able to dissuade Ivor from going to sea. Throughout the afternoon Ivor remained calm and normal for the first time since leaving Napsbury and the day ended happily with Ivor and his father walking back to Gloucester railway station to see Mr Chapman off.

As the months passed, with the help of his friends John Haines, the Gloucestershire poet, and Herbert Howells, Gurney's condition slowly improved. He walked many miles, either alone or in company with one of them, and found that in the countryside and

BOAR'S HILL,
OXFORD.

Oct 24.

Roebuck Yard is in Market Street, off the Cornmarket Street.

Dear Mr Harvey,

Many thanks for your letter.

Will you come to lunch with us at 1 p.m. on Sat, Nov 8th?

I hope that that will suit you comfortably.

There is a famous brake which leaves the Roebuck Hotel Yard at 12-30 daily. This will leave you close to my house in time for lunch. The driver will tell you how to proceed when he puts you down.

We look forward to meeting you both. With best greetings,

Yours very truly John Masefield.

Invitation from John Masefield to F.W. Harvey and Ivor Gurney

through physical exertion he could silence the 'voices' which tormented him.

By March 1919 he was fit enough to return to the Royal College of Music, this time to study with Dr Ralph Vaughan Williams.

In London, Gurney rented rooms first in Clifton Hill, St John's Wood, then in Winchester Road, Hampstead and finally, the cheapest, in Earls Court. Eventually he abandoned London lodgings altogether and moved out to 51 Queen's Road, High Wycombe. Here he resumed his organ post at Christ Church and his close friendship with the Chapmans. Now followed one of the happiest, most fruitful and creative periods in Gurney's life. In the second half of 1919 he set over forty songs and wrote a number of instrumental pieces in addition to writing many of his finest poems.

The Chapmans welcomed Gurney back as a son to their midst. The joy in family life, the countryside, home-cooking, music-making, boisterous fun and gentle pleasure provided the perfect atmosphere in which he could both relax and find inspiration. A second volume of verse, *Wars Embers*, was published by Sidgwick and Jackson. Gurney proudly presented a copy to: 'La Comtesse and the Chapman Family generally, with all good wishes for all sorts of good things from the Admiring Author. May 1919'. Of these poems Gurney dedicated 'The Battalion is Now at Rest' to 'La Comtesse'. 'The Poplar' to Micky and, to Winnie, 'The Immortal Hour'. Gurney's gifts to the Chapmans were usually books. For her birthday in August 1919 Winnie received the book which had been Ivor's trench companion – *The Path to Rome* by Hilaire Belloc – and for Christmas that year the play *Abraham Lincoln* by John Drinkwater.

Gurney slowly began to enjoy the recognition of poets whom he admired: Abercrombie, Shanks, Gibson and Bridges. In November 1919 Gurney and F.W. Harvey were invited to spend a day with John Masefield at his home near Oxford; Graves, Nichols and Bridges were there also. Masefield thought *War's Embers* very good. Given mental stability it seems likely that Gurney could now have begun to take his rightful place as a poet and composer of superb quality. Sadly, this was not to be.

Ivor Gurney with 'La Comtesse' and Micky in 1919.

As 1920 passed, Gurney spent less and less time at the R.C.M. and, to escape from London, resumed his long hikes into the countryside, even walking as far as Gloucester. He slept rough many times. The Chapmans became increasingly concerned about his unpredictable behaviour. On one occasion Gurney arrived at St. Michael's very late, after everyone had gone to bed. He entered the house through the kitchen window, raided the pantry and ate a tin of biscuits before falling asleep on a couch in the drawing room under Mr Chapman's overcoat. The following morning Mr Chapman came down to find Gurney lying on the couch surrounded by the remains of his irregular supper. In a sarcastic manner Mr Chapman offered Gurney the rest of the family's coats and the key to the cashbox. Gurney was distressed by what he had done and exclaimed: 'Oh dear, what an allotment!'

Ivor Gurney with 'La Comtesse' and Winnie in 1919.

In the summer of 1921 Gurney finally left the R.C.M. and returned to Gloucestershire to live with his aunt at Longford. Soon the dreadful voices in his head returned; and then a fear that he was being bombarded by radio waves. He left Longford and, without invitation, moved in with his brother and sister-in-law, Ronald and Ethel Gurney, who lived in Worcester Street, Gloucester. By 1922 Ivor's behaviour and eccentricity had grown intolerable to his family. He was certified insane and committed to Barnwood House, a mental hospital near Gloucester. However, he escaped from there, cutting his hands badly on broken glass in the process. It was decided that he should be committed to an asylum a long way from Gloucester and from which he could not escape. On 21 December 1922 he was taken to the City of London Mental Hospital at Dartford, Kent, there to remain for fifteen years until his death on 26 December 1937.

Album Leaf
For Nicky
Ivor Gurney

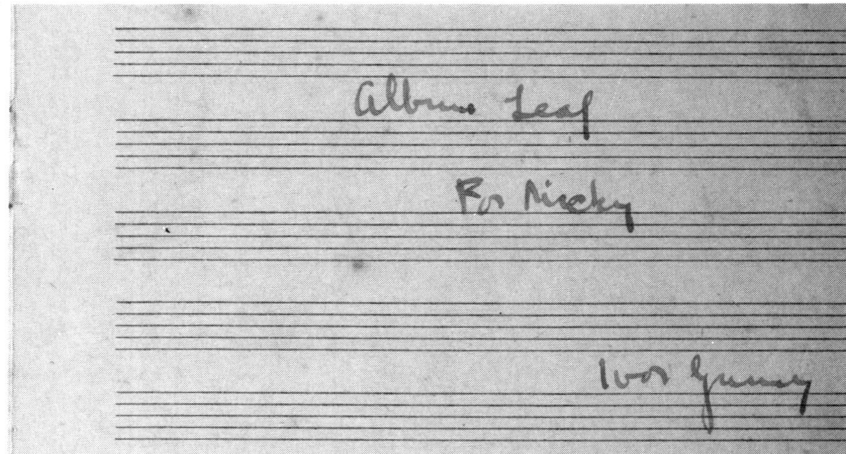

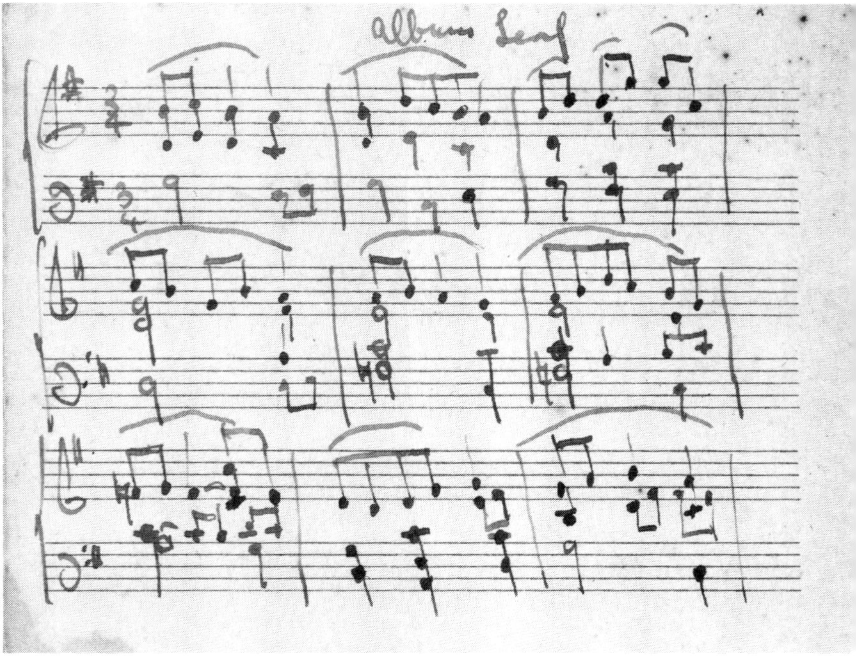

Album Leaf

October 1914

Chosen Hill, Churchdown, Gloucestershire.

In the introduction to his collection of Ivor Gurney's poems[1] Leonard Clark concluded: 'The pity is for Ivor Gurney himself whose generation did not know that he was burning and palpitating in their midst, with a fiery brain and heart, singing songs of the heart's pain and the world's loveliness, and hating what man's wars had done to man'. Indeed, if it had not been for the efforts of Marion Scott it is doubtful if any of Gurney's work would have survived at all. He sent her all his manuscripts and she had them typed out, retaining carbon copies and returning the originals to Gurney. It was she who arranged the publication of *Severn and Somme* and *War's Embers*; she too who first secured publication of any of his songs; and she it was who visited and tried to support him throughout the asylum years. However, she made no attempt to catalogue the mass of Gurney's work in her possession.

1. *Poems of Ivor Gurney*. Chatto and Windus (1973). Now out of print.

In spite of the approval received from established poets, such as Robert Bridges and Walter de la Mare, few of Gurney's poems appeared in print after 1919. It seems that his generation was indeed prepared to allow his work and the memory of him to fade into obscurity. Only one man was intent on rescue.

In 1920 the young composer Gerald Finzi heard the song 'Sleep' from Gurney's 'Five Elizas' sung by Elsie Suddaby with Sir Edward Bairstow the organist of York Minister. He felt it was one of the great songs, written with such intensity of feeling that it was like an electric light bulb that burns to brilliance before it explodes. This led him to discover Gurney and for the rest of his life, with the assistance of his friend Howard Ferguson, he worked to gather Gurney's poems and songs from every possible source. More songs were published and in 1954, two years before his death, Finzi initiated the publication of seventy-eight poems selected with an introduction by Edmund Blunden.[1]

The work which Finzi began has been continued by his widow Joy Finzi and the firm foundation upon which Gurney's reputation now stands is in large measure due to them. Amongst those who have built on that foundation are Leonard Clark, Charles W. Moore[2] and Gurney's biographer, Michael Hurd. Then, in 1982, as a result of painstaking research, P.J. Kavanagh was able to publish the most extensive collection of Gurney's poems to appear in print so far.[3] In addition, a selection of Gurney's war letters have been published by R.K.R. Thornton.[4]

And what of the Chapmans? In 1923 the Great Western Railway transferred Mr Chapman to the post of Goods Manager at Gloucester . . . Ivor's Gloucester. Eventually the family moved into Cranham House, Churchdown, at the foot of Chosen Hill where Gurney had walked with Herbert Howells, his friend since boyhood. Recollecting those walks and in memory of his friend, Howells dedicated his String Quartet in A minor: 'To the hill at

1. *Poems of Ivor Gurney*. Hutchinson (1954). Now out of print.
2. 'Ivor Gurney, A Lover and Maker of Beauty' a monograph by Charles W. Moore (Triad Press) 1976, 28pp.
3. *Collected Poems of Ivor Gurney*. (OUP) 1982. Paperback (revised) 1984.
4. *Ivor Gurney War Letters*. (Carcanet New Press) 1983. Paperback (Hogarth Press) 1984.

The Chapmans with a friend, Miss Colwell, at Cranham House, Churchdown.

Gerald Finzi

Chosen and Ivor Gurney who knew it'. (In later years Chosen Hill was the source of Gerald Finzi's *In Terra Pax*. It was here in the little church that he watched the bell ringers on New Year's Eve and afterwards joined them in the sexton's cottage nearby. The cantata was not completed for over twenty years and it was the last work which Finzi conducted in Gloucester shortly before his death).

Sadly the Chapmans missed seeing Ivor, who had already been taken to Dartford by the time they arrived in Gloucestershire. However, Mr Chapman visited him in the mental hospital on a number of occasions.

After the Spring of 1921 Ivor's visits to St Michael's had become less frequent. By now Kitty was married, and Winnie, Arthur and Micky had grown up. One day, after he had not been to see the Chapmans for some weeks, Winnie saw Ivor walking towards her as she rode her bicycle into High Wycombe. His face was full of despair. Winnie stopped her bicycle and said: 'Oh, Ivor, whatever is the matter?' Tears welled up in his eyes. Looking away, he made a little gesture of hopelessness with his hand and walked quickly on without a word. Winnie never saw him again.

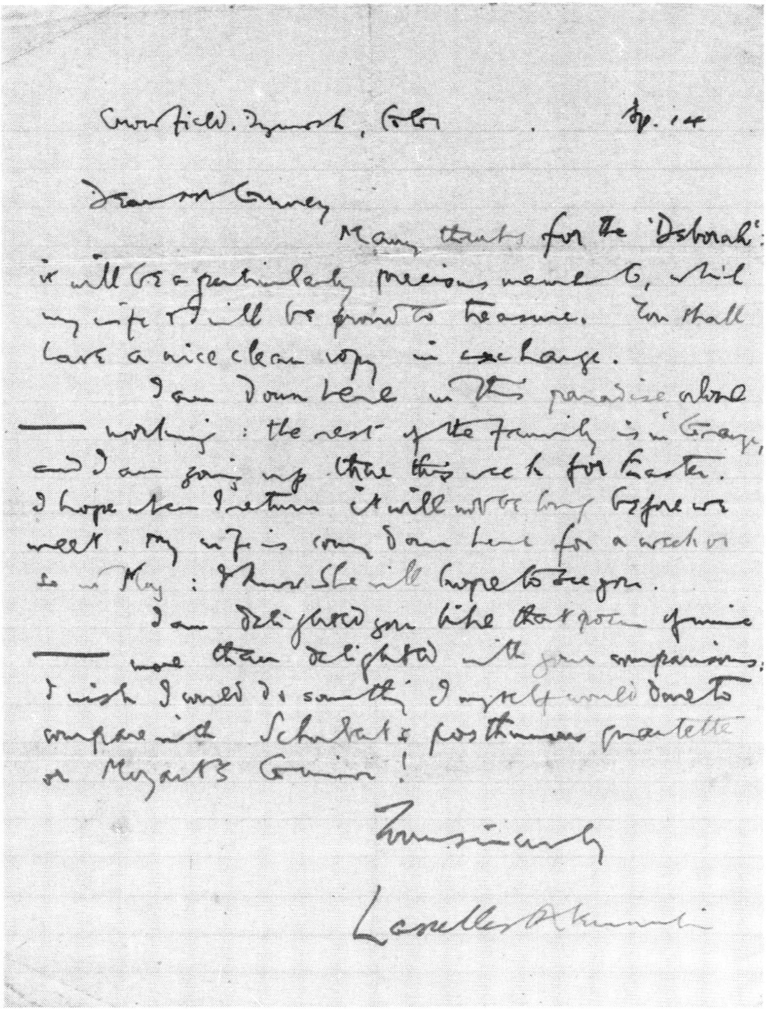

Crowsfield, Dymock, Glos. Ap. 14

Dear Mr Gurney

Many thanks for the 'Deborah': it will be a particularly precious memento, which my wife & I will be proud to treasure. You shall have a nice clean copy in exchange.

I am down here in this paradise alone — working: the rest of the family is in Grange, and I am going up there this week for Easter. I hope when I return it will not be long before we meet. My wife is coming down here for a week or so in May: & I know she will hope to see you.

I am delighted you like that poem of mine — more than delighted with your comparisons: I wish I could do something I myself would dare to compare with Schubert's posthumous quartette or Mozart's G minor!

Yours sincerely

Lascelles Abercrombie

Cloverfield, Dymock, Glos. Ap. 14

Dear Mr Gurney,

Many thanks for the 'Deborah': it will be a particularly precious memento, which my wife & I will be proud to treasure. You shall have a nice clean copy in exchange.

I am down here in this paradise alone – working: the rest of the family is in Grange, and I am going up there this week for Easter. I hope when I return it will not be long before we meet. My wife is coming down here for a week or so in May: I know she will hope to see you.

I am delighted you like that poem of mine – more than delighted with your comparisons: I wish I could do something I myself would dare to compare with Schubert's posthumous quartette or Mozart's G minor!

Yours sincerely,

Lascelles Abercrombie

To God

By Ivor Gurney

Why have you made life so intolerable
And set me between four walls, where I am able
Not to escape meals without prayer, for that is possible
Only by annoying an attendant. And tonight a sensual
Hell has been put upon me, so that all has deserted me
And I am merely crying and trembling in heart
For death, and cannot get it. And gone out is part
Of sanity. And there is dreadful hell within me.
And nothing helps. Forced meals there have been and electricity
And weakening of sanity by influence
That's dreadful to endure. And there is Orders
And I am praying for death, death, death,
And dreadful is the indrawing or outbreathing of breath
Because of the intolerable insults put on my whole soul,
Of the soul loathed, loathed, loathed of the soul.
Gone out every bright thing from my mind.
All lost that ever God himself designed.
Not half can be written of cruelty of man, on man,
Not often such evil guessed as between man and man.

5
'THE SPRINGS OF MUSIC'

An Essay
by
Ivor Gurney

IVOR GURNEY'S ESSAY 'THE SPRINGS OF MUSIC' WAS PUBLISHED IN THE UNITED STATES OF AMERICA IN 'THE MUSICAL QUARTERLY' OF JULY 1922. IT IS REPRODUCED IN FULL HERE FOR THE FIRST TIME IN THE UNITED KINGDOM.

THE MUSICAL QUARTERLY

O. G. SONNECK, *Editor*

VOL. 8, NO. 3 JULY, 1922

CONTENTS

PUBLISHED QUARTERLY

THREE DOLLARS A YEAR — At 3 East 43d Street New York, N. Y. — SEVENTY-FIVE CENTS A COPY

Entered as second-class matter December 31, 1914, at the Post Office at New York, N. Y., under the Act of March 3, 1879.

G. SCHIRMER, Inc. NEW YORK

THE SPRINGS OF MUSIC

By Ivor Gurney

Since the springs of music are identical with those of the springs of all beauty remembered by the heart, an essay with this title can be little more than a personal record of visions of natural fairness remembered, it may be, long after the bodily seeing.

It is the fact that these visions were more clearly seen after the excessive bodily fatigue experienced on a route march, or in some hard fatigue in France or Flanders – a compensation for so much strain. One found them serviceable in the accomplishment of the task, and in after-relaxation. There it was one learnt that the brighter visions brought music; the fainter verse, or mere pleasurable emotion.

Of all significant things the most striking, poignant, passioning, is the sight of a great valley at the end of the day – such as the Severn Valley which lies hushed and dark, infinitely full of meaning, while yet the far Welsh hills are touched with living and ecstatic gold. The first breakings of the air of night, the remembrance of the glory not all yet faded; the meeting of the two pageants of day and night so powerfully stir the heart that music alone may assuage its thirst, or satisfy that longing told by Wordsworth in the 'Prelude'; but that telling and outpouring of his is but the shadow and faint far-off indication of what Music might do – the chief use of Poetry seeming to be, to one, perhaps mistaken, musician, to stir his spirit to the height of music, the maker to create, the listener worthily to receive or remember.

The quietest and most comforting thing that is yet strongly suggestive – the sight which seems more than any to provoke the making of music to be performed on strings, is that of a hedge mounting over, rolling beyond the skyline of a little gracious hill. A hedge unclipped, untamed; covered with hawthorn perhaps, showing the fragile rose of June, or sombre with the bareness of Winter; the season makes no difference. So that the hedge be of some age and the hill friendly enough of aspect, smooth, strokable, as it were, there is no end to the quiet suggestion, the subdued yet still quick power of the sight.

What may not be taken from a road winding over against a West clear beneath, above crowned with dark angerful clouds? To walk there, having seen sunset pass – 'the brands of sunset fall, flicker and fade from out the West,' as a poet has said – to top the hill and take on his face the last of the sunset wind, the first of the night. And to pass on, see groups of quiet voiced cottagers talking at gates not iron but of friendly wood, surrounded by peace and a fragrance of honeysuckle or some such tender thing. This is to know where so much of Schumann's music had its source.

Beethoven comes with the majesty of a wide plain on a blowy day, ruled imperiously by hills but afar off – kingly-wise but in temperate fashion. A plain roofed by the blue and cloud dappled, gloriously changing, swept clean by wind loving yet rough, austere yet friendly. Or his is the sight of a heaven of stars, seen from high above the world; alone at midnight one must stand where long ago the Romans kept their watch, and knew either bare slopes or beech boughs sawing backwards and forwards against the dim blue and the starry points thereon. It is right that one who should wish to understand at least one of Beethoven's moods should wrap himself in one of the Master's moods on such a place as Painswick Beacon, when nothing human is abroad, not a light in the valley save in the distant town; when no sound comes to the bodily ear save that ghostly one of the owl.

A copse is full of infinite suggestion of Schubert, and if it were threaded by some tiny dancing stream running sunlit water like some strange and splendid metal. . . .

Birds talk and sing there, and the Unfinished symphony confirms one in wonder at the day's hotter hours.

Brahms has more of Autumn in him – the full coloured new ploughed earth also; rich-tinted, strongly fragrant soil unplanted. He has given us even the smell of leaves, it seems to myself at least; as in the Piano Quintet in F minor.

Orchards are the inspiration of so much; blossom has borne blossom of song so many times in so many men. 'Adelaide,' the First Rasoumoffsky Quartet, Schubert's songs, Schumann's songs and short pianoforte pieces, the songs of Brahms. . . . Who has not felt the spell of Spring so strongly symbolized herein?

As for the Sea, it has too little influenced or inspired the

Ivor Gurney at St. Michael's – 1919

Makers of Song. Vaughan Williams alone has worthily expressed his mood of glory at the scent, sound, sight of that infinite and unweakening wonder. The Germans seem to care little for the sea, and anyhow the centres that drew their great musicians were far enough from blue water. The mountains must supply that need of complete grandeur which thrusts a snowy peak high out of the score, even the notes read merely, of Eroica or Coriolanus.

In Bach is fairy tale, firelight, Cathedral space (of this a great deal), much human friendliness. The common intercourse of life, but raised high. An almost unparalleled grandeur is his at times, but seeming to come rather from ordered stone than the free majesty of mountain places, the sky or the sea. Yet such a man made out of talking sunlit water the Italian Concerto, and – as for the Chromatic Fantasia, of what was such a huge wonder born? Of sheer cliffs or a thought of the battle of good and evil in some mighty heart? None can say; it is with far more than the common gratitude that we accept such things. The Ninth Symphony begins with the mightiest of battle gatherings, and has the most tremendous of onslaughts in the few pages of its first movement. There the sky rages also as in King Lear; there the spirit of man realises its impotency yet eternal power of defiance before the forces of nature. Challenges, accepts and both powerfully, with dignity, and though certain in the end of doom, looks up at the ordered troops of dark cloud, and says, 'We are, but I shall be.'

From poplars has come much: the larch has given grace to thought in many of the smaller forms. The oak has strengthened many, and in the shady chambers of the elm many have found peace. Trees are the friendliness of things, and the beech with its smooth A major trunk, its laughing E major foliage; the Scotch fir which passionate or still is always F sharp minor, cannot have been without influence on men.

Autumn is strongest in memory of all the seasons. To think of Autumn is to be smitten through most powerfully with an F sharp minor chord that stops the breath, wrings the heart with unmeasurable power. On Brahms it is so strong, this royal season; has given him much, worthily and truly translated. What! do you not know the Clarinet Quintet, the Handel Variations, the C minor Symphony? And do you not smell Autumn air keen in the nostrils, touch and wonder at leaves fallen or about to fall? Have you not hastened to the woods of the F minor Quintet?

Perhaps you are too enamoured of the April of Mozart, in which you are both right and wrong. His is 'the cascade of the larch.' The young heavens forgetful after rain. Arcady is his, and in the springing season.

Children are always a delight, but the large eyes and innocence of them are not Mozart's only, but of Schubert, Schumann, Haydn, and almost supremely of Bach, when he chooses to be fascinated by them. What is the little Prelude and Fugue in G major in the second part of the '48,' but a fairy tale for children?

And who but a child brought the A major Concerto to us, or the F sharp Piano Sonata? (Of Mozart and Beethoven.)

Firelight is infinitely strong on us all, but on Schumann pre-eminently. One would think that man to have known Cotswold, and to have sheltered from its winter air in a house built of the stone most worthily used for Cathedrals, and as perfectly built. To have watched the dance and interlacing of shadows on the dim walls, but most to have gazed and lost himself in the deepest heart of the log-fire roaring upwards towards the vast chimney and the frosty stars.

This queer discursive essay-thing has come from remembrance of natural beauty which has brought music, and of music that opened suddenly a pathway through to show some picture, long ago seen, it may be, but passioned, made mystic and far more dear from the unexpectedness of the gift. A beauty out of beauty suddenly thrust unasked upon a heart that dared not want more; had not dreamed of asking more, and was suddenly given completely eternal right in Cranham, Portway, Redmarley, Crickley – before, the Paradise of Earth; after, as things unearthly, not to be thought on without tears, nor a fear of loss known deep in the spirit to be unfounded, unbelievable.

Worse nonsense has been written about such things as we all believe, and though truth is better treated more honestly, yet even through this mist of pretty words may show some of the plainness of the truth as it may have seemed to the makers and receivers.

The Songs I Had

By Ivor Gurney

The songs I had are withered
Or vanished clean,
Yet there are bright tracks
Where I have been

And there grow flowers
For others' delight.
Think well, O singer,
Soon comes night.